DRIFT

"In a *dérive*, one or more persons during a certain period drop their relations, their work and leisure activities, and all their other usual motives for movement and action, and let themselves be drawn by the attractions of the terrain and the encounters they find there."
— Guy Debord, *Theory of the Dérive,* 1958.

The translation of *dérive* is *drift*.

MANHATTAN

DEAR READER,

For our tenth issue of *Drift*, we return to our hometown of New York City, and zoom in to where our humble coffee chronicles began: the borough of Manhattan. An international capital of culture and finance, Manhattan's mix of languages and cuisines, lifestyles and perspectives—roughly two million inhabitants from all walks of life live on this small, densely packed island—is what makes this grid of skyscrapers, the largest of New York City's five boroughs, so unique. But, this year, a deadly pandemic from a novel coronavirus took the world by storm and impacted New York City particularly harshly. The city's resilience was also tested in a tumultuous season of demonstrations that followed, spurred by a racial justice movement and growing frustrations with government.

We began compiling this issue at the height of the coronavirus outbreak, when lockdowns changed the look and feel of the city. Early morning sidewalks, once crowded with commuters drinking coffee, were replaced with emptiness: signs that read "MASKS REQUIRED" and social distancing markers appeared everywhere to remind us of a grim, new reality. Storefront windows in SoHo were shattered in civil unrest, and in many areas graffiti covered street signs with sharp, political messages. Almost all of our favorite coffee shops closed or limited service.

But as we started to wrap up the editing process a few months later, we noticed the city slowly beginning the process of reopening and rehabilitating. It is a testament to the irrepressible spirit and strength of our fellow New Yorkers.

In this special edition of *Drift*, we felt it important to show love and solidarity with our home, a place which has been heavily affected by this year's events. Volume 10: Manhattan celebrates this city that never sleeps, taking the reader from the mid-1800s, when coffee roasting was once abundant in Manhattan's Financial District, to the present day, highlighting nostalgic moments throughout which make this city so irresistible. We explore how local shops and businesses are evolving to survive rent hikes and a changing urban landscape. From the history of the city's iconic "We Are Happy To Serve You" to-go cups and the classic black and white cookie, to innovative drinks at a locomotive-inspired coffee shop in Midtown Manhattan, we explore old and new.

Our writers and photographers left footprints from Harlem all the way down to the Financial District, canvassing the diverse pockets of international culture in between for flat whites, Ethiopian cold brew, charcoal-roasted coffee, and *pão di queijo*. Whether it is during the morning commute, at a first date, at a coffee cart, or in a diner or third-wave shop, coffee is ever-present in the life of Manhattanites. Pour a hot cup of coffee and join us in the retelling of their stories in *Drift*, Volume 10: Manhattan.

ADAM GOLDBERG,
EDITOR IN CHIEF

One Sharp Cookie

WORDS
Georgie Carroll

PHOTOGRAPHS
Daniela Velasco

Like any comestible classic, the black-and-white cookie is a conversation piece. But more than the bagel, the pizza, or the cheesecake, the black-and-white's success is in its power to keep New Yorkers talking about it.

The flat shortbread round, with its familiar half-chocolate, half-vanilla glazed top, has its provenance in New York City. It's thought to be one of the early offerings at Glaser's Bake Shop on the Upper East Side, founded by Bavarian immigrants in 1902. The black-and-white is much bigger than an ordinary cookie, about four inches across. The basic recipe, according to Jennifer Brizzi in "Savouring Gotham" (2015) is sugar, eggs, flour, sometimes milk, vanilla, and lemon extract (maybe orange), with a frosting of confectioner's sugar, water, bitter chocolate, and a bit of corn syrup.

The black-and-white divides the people in its own image with the question of whether it's a cookie at all. Former food critic at The New York Times Molly O'Neill writes: "They are the runes of deli counters and bakeries. Why? Because they are not what they appear to be. Black-and-white cookies are not even cookies. They are floury cakes baked in a cookie style." Although Sam Roberts admits that the black-and-white barely qualifies as a cookie in his impassioned "A History of New York in 100 Objects" (2014), he fights for it over other iconic edibles because somehow "It democratically says New York."

You'll find the black-and-white at almost every deli and bakery in New York City. Across Manhattan there are shrink-wrapped avatars in bodegas and chain cafes. The cake-like round has even appeared, tongue-in-cheek, on a $195 tasting menu at the three Michelin-starred restaurant Eleven Madison Park, suggesting that the *idea* of the black-

RUSS&DAUGHTERS
THU
FRI
SAT
SUN
CURED SALMON
SMOKED FISH
SABLE
STURGEON
WHITEFISH - WHOLE
WHITEFISH FILLETED
CHUBS
BROOK TROUT
YELLOWFIN TUNA
PEPPERED MACKEREL
RUSS & DAUGHTERS
Black and White Cookie
(PCS)
2
Appetizing Since 1914

GENUINE NOVA
KAPCHUNKAS
SMOKED EEL
APPETIZERS
PLEASE DO
NOT TOUCH
SURFACES

APPETIZING SINCE 1914
& DAUGHTERS OCCUPIES THAT RARE AND
PLACE ON THE MOUNTAINTOP RESERVED FOR
OSE WHO ARE NOT JUST THE OLDEST AND
LAST – BUT ALSO THE BEST
– ANTHONY BOURDAIN
– HALVAH – RUGELACH – DRIED FRUIT – NUTS
CANDY – EGG CREAMS
SHIP NATIONWIDE & DELIVER IN NYC
wRUSSANDDAUGHTERS.COM
TED NUTS
IMPORTED CANDIES
GOLDEN RAISINS
SEEDLESS RAISINS
PITTED PRUNES
HONEY ROASTED PECANS
RAW PECANS
RAW WALNUTS
ROASTED ALMONDS
RAW ALMONDS
BLUEBERRIES
GOOSEBERRIES
TART CHERRIES
PAPAYA
BANANAS
PINEAPPLE
TURKISH APRICOTS
MANGO

RUSS &
APPET
179
SMOKED EEL
KAPCHUNKAS
105 YEARS
RUSS&DAUGHTERS
BE A MENSCH.
WEAR A MASK.
STURGEON
GREEK
For Pre-Orders
Line up to your Left
Masks Required
Two (2) Customers
allowed inside at once
Masks Required
Line up to your Right
to wait your turn
PUSH
RUSS&DAUGHTERS
OPEN 7 DAYS A WEEK
9am - 4pm
RUSS&DAUGHTERS

and-white has outgrown its form. It is more than a cookie. It's a piece of history, a mouthful of the city itself. Having achieved icon status, it is recognizable even when modified. Long-standing kosher bakery William Greenberg's, synonymous with the monochromatic treat, sells kaleidoscopic color combinations too (and one with a red velvet cake base). Black-and-whites occasionally come in miniature sizes. And often, the split-down-the-middle design is applied with varying degrees of exactitude, depending on where you buy them.

The most sought-out and freshest black-and-whites are sold at busy kosher bakeries. O'Neill writes that the cookie at Zabar's on Broadway "is to the deli version what pâté is to chopped liver." What makes a black-and-white good is as disputed as its status as a cookie. There's something to be said for a tasty glaze using real chocolate and vanilla. However, the black-and-white is, above all, an object of nostalgia. Tasters want tradition, or more precisely, a memory. And maybe that memory *is* of a cookie with a glaze that's mass-produced, a chocolate that tastes cheap.

Glaser's used to make black-and-whites with a fluffy frosting rather than the more typical glaze. The bake shop was the last of its kind to close in 2018. It had become an institution, famed for Bavarian pastries and legendary black-and-whites. Its preserved storefront spoke of the days when Yorkville was known as Germantown, streets lined with German butchers, bakers, and restaurants and 86th Street was nicknamed "Sauerkraut Boulevard." Many of the area's inhabitants had relocated there from "Little Germany" in what is now the East Village, and poorer immigrants were moving in. Joel Russ arrived in New York from Poland in 1907, and after selling schmaltz herring out of a barrel to Eastern European Jews on the Lower East Side, eventually opened Russ & Daughters at 179 East Houston Street, in 1920. Today it sells arguably the best black-and-whites in the city, alongside a matching sundae made of cookie batter ice cream, half-coated in a chocolate shell.

The original German cookie was all white. Re-iced in its current form, it is thought to have been reintroduced to Germany by the American army in the 1950s, where, in the former West Germany it was called *amerikaner*. (Anti-American sentiment in East Germany led to the less appetizing moniker 'ammonia cookies' or *ammonplätzchen*.)

There's no real explanation for the two-toned concept, though "MoonPies, scooter pies, and whoopie pies [were] popularized during the same period" ("The Oxford Companion to Sugar and Sweets"), which, like the Oreo (born in 1912), were also light and dark desserts. Contrasting color dominated the art and design of the time too. To say that the black-and-white was a nod to the Art Deco semi-circle might be far-fetched. But perhaps it's not far-fetched to say that it tapped into a certain aesthetic. The frosting definitely doesn't seem out of place in a visual world where bold, geometric forms were fashionable. The use of stark contrast and half circles by modernist artists at the time feel relevant, as do the graphic shapes and use of bold, opposing colors in the golden age of poster design in Europe from the 1890s to 1910s.

Structuralist theory, developing in the early 1900s in Europe, was also interested in polarity as fundamental to human thought. The black-and-white appeals to the most primitive parts of our minds. Maybe this is why it is so unforgettable, why there is something hypnotic about it. It won't be the first time the cookie has been likened to yin and yang; a system that reduces the world into opposites: feminine and masculine, water and fire, day and night. (Some say the black-and-white descends from the "half-moon cookie," apparently first made at Hemstrought's Bakery in Utica, in Upstate New York. But it's unclear which came first. The names are sometimes used interchangeably, though the half-moon is smaller, made of devil's food cake, and has a fluffy, buttercream frosting.)

In recent decades the cookie has been interpreted as a racial metaphor. In 2008, Obama called them "unity cookies" during a presidential campaign, echoing the famous scene in a 1994 episode of "Seinfeld." "Nothing mixes better," Jerry tells Elaine, "than vanilla and chocolate. And yet, somehow, racial harmony eludes us. If only people would look to the cookie, all our problems would be solved." "Seinfeld" shot the black-and-white to national fame, making it available at chain coffee shops nationwide. Still, the cookie's home is New York City, where it can be found at select (as well as chain) coffee houses, such as Danny Meyer's bakery/cafe Daily Provisions in Union Square. In 2019, Manhattan's Magnolia Bakery, which popularized the cupcake on "Sex and the City," sold a limited edition black-and-white to honor the 30th anniversary of "Seinfeld." The bakery has since added it to its permanent menu.

Some claim that the cookie's symmetry provides a peaceful antidote to the chaos of the city. Then again, it could represent the opposite, a city constantly in flux. The cookie eludes us—whatever it is, it also is not. It is neither entirely black nor white, neither cake nor cookie. It can be fancy or cheap, kitsch or profound. It's a kind of riddle, a morsel of irony, which seems to have infinite meaning. If the black-and-white cookie is one thing and one thing alone, it is relevant.

–

Taking One's Coffee Black

WORDS
Jonathan Shipley

ILLUSTRATION
Nell Hugh-Jones

POSTER DESIGN
Jojo Anavim

A boy from Lithuania had dreams of being an engineer. He worked nights in New York City to pay for his education. Graduating from Columbia University in 1926, he had the American Dream in his head and $250 in his pocket. But engineering jobs didn't come easy for the Lithuanian. So, on the corner of Broadway and 43rd Street, William Black set up a stand and started selling nuts.

Black sold so many roasted nuts that he began turning a profit, and eventually, expanded his business. Within six years he had 18 small stores throughout the city. He called his company Chock Full o'Nuts.

When the Great Depression hit, "roasted nuts were a bit of a luxury item, and [were] no longer affordable to the average working person," notes Brian Kubicki, a Vice President of Chock Full o'Nuts. Passers-by started passing Black by. "Mr. Black began looking for new ways to use the assets he already owned and decided to begin roasting coffee." Black already had the stores, and he already had roasters. "The rest, as they say, is history." Black converted his shops into lunch counters in the early 1930s. For a nickel one could get a nutted sandwich—cream cheese and chopped nuts on slices of dark raisin bread—and a cup of coffee.

By the 1950s Black was selling his coffee in grocery stores throughout New York. His empire was growing, and he was forging high-profile relationships. "At some point late in his career with the Dodgers, Jackie Robinson became friends with Mr. Black," Kubicki says. "Around the time the Dodgers moved to Los Angeles, Mr. Black offered Jackie a job as Vice President of Personnel." For Mr. Black, it wasn't just to get a star into the Chock Full o'Nuts executive team. "Mr. Black and his company were already regarded as one of the most progressive, for the time, in terms of hiring practices. Robinson was the perfect ambassador to manage employee relations." Ninety percent of Black's workforce were Black. Employees, from the executives to the sandwich makers, received sickness and medical insurance, pension plans, interest-free loans, profit sharing, and bonuses.

Black's coffee accounted for 60% of the company's revenue in 1960. It only went up from there, especially after Chock Full o'Nuts debuted its instant coffee in 1961. Within a decade, the company had about 80 shops throughout the city. "If you ask any New Yorker from that era where they had breakfast," Kubicki says, "they would likely name one of these three places: Five & Dime stores, Horn and Hardart, or Chock Full o'Nuts."

Though the stand-alone shops have dwindled considerably from their 1960s heyday, the brand and its coffee sales have not. Today Chock Full o'Nuts is owned by Italy-based Massimo Zanetti Beverage Group, the largest privately owned coffee company in the world. But to be clear, despite the company's name, its coffee doesn't (and never has) contained nuts. It's now clearly labeled that way—100% nut-free. "We take pride," Kubicki says, "in consistency cup to cup, can to can, batch to batch, and year to year."

It has been nearly a 100 years since Chock Full o'Nuts was founded. Black passed away in 1983 of cancer. There's no telling what he'd think of the company now, one he started on a street corner when he couldn't get a job after college. There's a Chock Full o'Nuts commercial jingle from the 1960s. It had these lyrics: "Chock Full o'Nuts is that heavenly coffee, heavenly coffee, heavenly coffee. Chock Full o'Nuts is that heavenly coffee, better coffee Rockefeller's money can't buy." And yet, with only $250 in his pocket, Black bought himself more than just heavenly coffee. He bought himself the American Dream.

–

Chock full o'Nuts
Chock full o'Nuts
Chock full o'Nuts

Chock full o' Nut
REG. U.S. PAT. OFF.
LIBERTY

"Indulge"
Jojo Anavim
56x36in
Mixed media on panel

Inspired by old New York City coffee billboards in the sixties.

Blurring the line between mass consumerism and fine art, New York City based artist Jojo Anavim has established his body of work stemming from a background in graphic design and consumer marketing. His work blends the mechanical process of his design roots with a vibrant palate and vivid brush strokes of acrylic and oil paint.

IT'S OUR
PLEASURE
TO SERVE
YOU

Long Live the Anthora Cup

WORDS
Sabrina Sucato

PHOTOGRAPHS
Adam Goldberg, Daniela Velasco

You've seen it before.

Even if you didn't know its name, you recognized it as a vessel for the lifeblood of Manhattan. You've observed it at diners, where swirls of steam pipe off just-poured java, and spotted it at coffee carts, where commuters, locals, and everyone in between line up for that requisite cup of joe to sustain them until they're ready to rise and grind all over again. Perhaps you even noticed it in the hands of Detective Olivia Benson on "Law & Order: Special Victims Unit" or Don Draper in "Mad Men," two shows as deeply entrenched in New York City as the prop in question.

What is it?

It's the Anthora cup, and it's a tough one to spot these days.

But let's rewind first.

More than 50 years before the iconic blue-and-white cup emblazoned with the words "We Are Happy To Serve You" made its debut in New York City, there were coffee carts. Rolling up to the city's industrial hubs toward the end of the 19th century, the earliest coffee carts were more along the lines of food wagons, popping up to supply workers with coffee, tea, and simple sustenance after restaurants closed shop for the day. By the time the Great Depression tore its way across the nation, street carts were a saving grace for residents who lived on pinched pennies.

Now fast-forward 30-odd years to 1963, when Leslie Buck invented the cup that would appeal to a city of immigrants and up-and-comers. Then Marketing Director for Sherri Cup Co., Buck was no stranger to adaptation and innovation. In his earlier years, the Czechoslovakian native survived the Holocaust, then relocated to New York City before

RESSO $2.50
ERICANO $2.75
ACHIATO $3.00
ORTADO $3.25
APPUCINO $3.50
FLAT WHITE $3.50
LATTE $3.50, 4.00
COFFEE
2.50, 3.00
ICED COFFEE $3.25, 3.75, 4.25
CHAI $3.50, 4.00
ICED ADD 50¢
EXTRA SHOT $1.00
MOCHA ADD 50¢
PEDDLER

NYU
ESPRESSO
AMERICANO
CAPPUCCINO
FLAT WHITE
COFFEE
ICED COFFEE
HOT CHOCOLATE
CHAI

Byron Kaplan

ultimately forging a career in the paper cup business. By the time the '60s rolled around, Buck recognized that the company had the potential to expand its presence within the American Northeast. It just needed the right hook.

Enter the Anthora cup. The product of copious research on Buck's part, the blue-and-white cup was initially a lure for New York's Greek-owned diners. With a coloration inspired by the Greek flag, a Greek key design bordering the rim, and a Greek amphora jar on the sides near the "We are happy to serve you" text, the cup was dubbed "Anthora" as a reference to Buck's mispronunciation of "amphora."

Design in hand, Buck and Sherri Cup Co. introduced the Anthora to New York City and, more specifically, to the city's Greek immigrants and their diners and coffee carts. In no time at all, the cup was an omnipresent fixture in Manhattan.

"For the pedestrian, and for those in a hurry to get back to the office, there was the coffee cart, a city-licensed enterprise where you could grab a cup on the go," explains Donald Schoenholt, President of Gillies Coffee Company, the oldest coffee merchant still in existence in America. A lifelong New Yorker and coffee historian who keeps a porcelain version of the cup permanently on his desk, Schoenholt recalls the early days of the cup's debut in Manhattan. "Many of these peddlers and many of the coffee shop operators were Greek Americans, and they looked to men who shared their heritage as suppliers."

Over the years, beginning right around when "Mad Men's" Bob Benson would have handed Don Draper a cup of coffee in the show's sixth season, the Anthora's popularity skyrocketed. And its popularity continued for nearly 30 years, with sales topping 500 million cups in 1994. By that time, the cup was so firmly ingrained into Manhattan's coffee culture that it seemed nothing could tear it away.

Then a few things happened. The same year the Anthora cup reached its peak, the very first Starbucks in Manhattan opened on 87th and Broadway. Just over 10 years later in 2005, Solo Cup Co. bought Sherri Cup Co. By that time, sales had declined to 200 million cups per year. Recognizing the drop in popularity, Solo put a halt on much of the distribution, opting instead to sell the design license that would later appear as change purses, cufflinks, and ceramic sets in venues like MoMA's gift store.

In the span of 10 years, the Anthora cup grew rarer and rarer in a landscape dominated by the green and white siren logo. Coffee carts and diners ordered other cups, sometimes going with what was cheaper, sometimes opting for alternative and eco-friendly materials. When Dart Container Corp. purchased Solo Cup Co. in 2012, Manhattan was a city of coffeehouse franchises, with the cups to match.

All the while, the memory of the Anthora cup, which The New York Times named in its "A History of New York in 50 Objects" feature, lingered. It lingered so much that, in 2015, Dart Container Corp. reincarnated it as a real-deal solution to the knockoff competitors on the market. Nowadays, the cup, which is available in both 8 and 10 oz. sizes, and is crafted from plant-based renewable materials with a polyethylene lining, is available exclusively to coffee carts, diners, and restaurants in Dart Container Corp.'s Region One market, which includes New York City and northeastern states. In other words, you won't find very many original versions on the West Coast.

"More than any other sign or symbol, the SOLO Anthora™ cup means *coffee* to every New Yorker," observes Margo Burrage, Director of Corporate Communications at Dart Container Corp. "It's identified with independent, hard-working small business owners who are 'happy to serve' their local communities."

Even though the Anthora cup might no longer be as visibly present in Manhattan as it once was (although, Burrage notes, sales were trending upward prior to the COVID-19 pandemic), its status as an icon remains, lingering into the present day via guest appearances everywhere from "Billions" to "The Sopranos" to "Suits." For Byron Kaplan, owner of concept coffee cart company Peddler, the cup is as integral to the city as coffee carts themselves.

"I think [the Anthora cup] will always exist in one form or another," he observes, adding that its function is a utilitarian one, and one that echoes back to the lasting presence of the delis, diners, and coffee carts from which the cup originates. Like the cup, he notes that coffee carts are "intrinsic to the social fabric of the streets. Each one is its own microcosm of New York City life."

In fact, it was Kaplan's Greek heritage combined with his passion for Manhattan's longstanding coffee culture that ultimately led him to design a cup for Peddler that he named "Adonis." A fusion of the Peddler logo and American flag in Greek key, the cup pays homage to the same Greek roots that the Anthora does.

"The Greek key came about from staring at the bottom of a piña colada at Connolly's in the Rockaways [in Queens]," he explains. "Greek key is all over the city, particularly on the older subway platforms."

While Kaplan's cup is a modernized take on those same cultural references that first influenced Buck, his is one that, like the Anthora itself, plays the same serviceable role for contemporary New Yorkers as the Anthora did for Tommy Lee Jones in "Men in Black" or for busy commuters on the way to work in the 1980s. It's attractive enough to feel like a step up from plain paper, but nothing so sacred as to make it more valuable than the contents inside. It is, after all that, simply a coffee cup.

–

AU CHOCOLAT
CROISSANT

A Shining Gargantua

WORDS
Jonathan Shipley

IIIUSTRATION
John Donohue

The cappuccino harkens to the Capuchin friary founded in 1525 under the Order of the Friars Minor by Matteo de Bascio when he was inspired by God to return to a life of solitude and penance first exemplified by Francis of Assisi. "The characteristic simplicity of these friars is, indeed, proverbial; and it may, too, be inferred from their speech, their manners, and from their very aspect," wrote Algernon Taylor in "Scenes in French Monasteries in 1746." "Besides being further illustrated by several sayings current in Italy—where their order is numbered by the thousand—such as 'to dine al cappuccino,' to make but a sorry meal."

When the first cappuccino drink was introduced in Italy it was named after the Capuchin friars because the color of the espresso mixed with frothed milk was similar to the color of the friars' robes. The name stuck. It came into the English language in the late 1800s and no one has been sorry for it since.

The cappuccino came to America by way of Italian Domenico Parisi, a patron saint of hot beverages. He opened and owned Caffe Reggio in New York City's Greenwich Village. It was 1927, and with an ornate chrome and bronze espresso machine, Parisi served a New Yorker the first cappuccino in America. The drink stuck and the espresso machine, long-retired, still sits in the cafe, a cafe that is still abuzz with the making of coffee and community. "The espresso machine is still in working condition," notes Fabrizio Cavallacci, the cafe's current owner.

"Dominic's Espresso machine is a shining Gargantua," noted the New York Herald Tribune in 1945 in an article touting the cafe. "Equipped with many spigots, filled with hot water and steam, which makes a cup of coffee in just about three seconds." Dominic Parisi spent his life savings, $1,000, to import the machine from Italy. His life was spent as a barber, before turning his attention to the cafe. He would serve coffee to folks waiting for their turn in the barber chair. The machine was made in 1902 for a World's Fair. The machine's domed top is crowned by a statuette of an angel, and the base is surrounded by dragons. It is an impressive marriage of engineering and design.

Parisi made a rule that only he could touch it. "He rubs it with loving care," the news article continued. "With it he makes a strong black coffee or a cappuccino (a marvelous blend of strong coffee, steaming milk, and cinnamon). 'Real' coffee lovers haunt his cafe."

And real coffee lovers still do, from locals down the street, to tourists from all corners of the globe; from folks with a few dollars in their pockets to the rich and renowned. "We have many famous people come by," Cavallacci says. "I never keep track of them." At 119 MacDougal Street in Greenwich Village, it's been a haunt for celebrities for decades. The Beat Generation sipped cappuccinos there, including Kerouac enjoyed his cup of joe at a corner table. The cafe was in such movies as "The Godfather Part II," "Shaft," and "Inside Llewyn Davis." And President John F. Kennedy made a campaign stop there in 1959.

Kennedy must have marveled at the espresso machine like the writer of a 1955 New Yorker article. The machine was "one of the biggest and most frightening urns in the Village. Frightening because, in drawing a cappuccino, he releases a valve which allows steam to whip milk into a froth and emit an appalling, ripping sound, like a barrage of rockets fired from a dive bomber." But, oh, the taste of that freshly brewed cup of coffee.

Originally, the machine ran on coal. Then, in the 1970s, Niso and Hilda Cavallacci, Fabrizio's parents, converted the machine to gas power. "My mother bought Reggio in 1955 from Parisi. I've never ever closed the place in 50 years," Fabrizio says proudly. "I had to for one month and a half because of COVID."

Open, Caffe Reggio is again, for people to imbibe hot beverages and take in the richly patinated atmosphere (one that includes a painting from the school of Caravaggio; a bench once owned by the de' Medici family in the 1400s; and a ceiling fan that was a prop in the movie "Casablanca"). What does the future hold for the cafe, as the angel atop Parisi's espresso machine still looks skyward? Fabrizio Cavallacci has some heavenly ideas. "Make people enjoy the atmosphere of Caffe Reggio for ever and ever."

Amen to that.

–

CAFFE REGGIO ORIGINAL CAPPUCCINO
ORIGINAL CAPPUCCINO
SINCE 1927

Right To Roast

WORDS
Sabrina Sucato

PHOTOGRAPHS
Adam Goldberg, Daniela Velasco

Coffee is everywhere in Manhattan. From the early dawn to well past the witching hour, it courses through the veins of the city that never sleeps. It's the lifeblood of the island, offering sustenance from every bodega, cafe, and aluminum-sided cart that lines the city's streets.

Yet, while the beverage—not to mention the innumerable venues from which to purchase it—is omnipresent in New York, the roasting facilities that give green beans their toasty brown hue are not. Ironically, when it comes to roasteries in Manhattan, the city is a veritable ghost town.

Why? In a city where possibility has much to do with determination, dollars, and a dream, it would seem that opening a roastery would come down to two requirements: a roasting permit and sufficient space. While both are theoretically possible to achieve—the first via paperwork and the second through a fair amount of scouting and funds—the reality of roasting in Manhattan is littered with roadblocks that, more often than not, offer wide-open exits to places like Brooklyn, Queens, and Jersey City, where the air is open and restrictions for environmental protection and zoning are relatively lighter.

In Manhattan, the near impossibility of roasting is a two-fold dilemma. The first and greatest deterrence has to do with New York City's Department of Environmental Protection, the organization that supplies permits for the installation and operation of coffee roasters, and its efforts to limit air pollution in a congested city. Because coffee roasting results in a noticeable, somewhat pungent odor (remember this is not fully roasted coffee, which smells something like heaven on earth), it can be cause for complaint mere minutes after the first scents of toasted beans waft outside. The second stumbling block relates to zoning and, more specifically, the space that roasting machines require to operate safely. Depending on how significant production is, roasters generally need to be zoned for manufacturing and possess roasters outfitted with afterburners. With an increasingly scarce number of lots still zoned

Ninth Street Espresso

Jeb Allred

SUSTAINABLE C

LORING

 Nina Glikshtern

for manufacturing in Manhattan, it's ultimately more affordable, more environmentally viable, and far less of a headache to roast in the outer boroughs or beyond.

It wasn't always this way. When the first commercial roasteries hit the scene in the mid-1800s, they brought with them a wealth of opportunity and industry. Instead of roasting green beans at home, Gotham residents became increasingly accustomed to purchasing pre-roasted coffee instead. Their demand for coffee led to a boom in roasting from the 1860s to the 1880s. By the early 1900s, the demand led to the creation of New York City's very own Coffee District.

Located in the area that today encircles Water Street in the Financial District, the Coffee District was a hub for roasteries like Kobrick Coffee Company and Gillies Coffee Company, the latter of which remains the oldest coffee merchant in the nation. Yet, with the arrival of the World's Fair in 1964-65, city officials recognized the need to change the downtown landscape to better accommodate pedestrians and, with them, commerce.

"By the mid 70s to the early 80s there were no commercial roasters on the island of Manhattan," explains Erin Meister, author of "New York City Coffee: A Caffeinated History." According to her, it was a combination of city ordinances to widen Water Street, near to where many coffee factories were located, and the ever-increasing cost of rent that ultimately pushed holdouts like Gillies to Brooklyn and Kobrick to Jersey City, where there were fewer restrictions on commercial roasting.

By the early 90s, roasters in the heart of New York City were a rarity. Porto Rico Importing Co. on Bleeker Street was grandfathered into the city's shifting landscape, although it too now roasts in Brooklyn, with retail locations in Manhattan. For the most part, however, the major players were left to restart operations in other boroughs. For newcomers to the scene, even taking a look at potential roasting facilities in Manhattan was a losing battle from the outset.

"Initially, we looked at possible locations in Manhattan," admits Chris Calkins, CEO and Founder of Gotham Coffee Roasters, which took root in 2013. "To really do a serious roasting facility, it takes a lot of space, and real estate is such a premium here."

Calkins settled upon Brooklyn, where he continues to roast about 5,000 pounds a month. He's joined by neighbors like Cafe Grumpy, which began roasting in 2009, and City of Saints Roasting Company, which debuted its Bushwick roastery in 2014. While Brooklyn is desirable for its proximity to Manhattan cafes, it isn't a one-size solution for all. For Irving Farm's owners, for instance, New York City's roasting restrictions led them not to the boroughs, but further upstate.

"In 1998, once we purchased our roaster, we went looking in Brooklyn because we were told we'd have a lot of trouble in the city," notes co-founder Stephen Leven. Yet after striking out on the real estate front, Leven and partner David Elwell looked north to the Hudson Valley, where they found their perfect digs at an old farm in Millerton. Nowadays, they operate three different roasting machines with the potential to churn out about 50,000 pounds a month to fuel their seven coffee shops, most of which are in New York City.

Yet in a city that's endlessly evolving and reinventing itself, sooner or later someone finds a way to make the seemingly impossible possible. Case in point: Ninth Street Espresso's Ken Nye successfully maneuvered a Loring S15 Falcon roaster into his Chelsea Market space because it's still zoned as an M1 light manufacturing district, thanks to its former days as a Nabisco factory. Another example is Roasting Plant, the concept coffee brand on the Lower East Side known for its patented Javabot micro-roasting technology. This machine, which is designed for single-serve, on-demand use—allowing customers to select their preferred single-origin bean or blend for a fresh cup of coffee—doesn't roast at large scale, and therefore isn't prohibited by regulations.

And then there's Starbucks. When the chain debuted its New York Roastery less than a block down the road from Ninth Street Espresso at the end of 2018, it did so with fanfare and more funding than one might want to imagine. A behemoth in Chelsea, the Roastery lives up to its namesake with its custom Probat roaster and massive degassing cask. Yet unlike the roasteries in the outer boroughs of New York City, where the primary purpose is production, this Starbucks roastery focuses on educating visitors, and not on producing coffee beans for customers across the globe.

Not that that's a bad thing, however.

"Let the Starbucks of the world have Manhattan," Meister observes. In her mind, the presence of roasteries in less trafficked areas of Brooklyn and Queens is a boon to the development of coffee culture overall. "You don't hear about specialty coffee in Flushing. Maybe if [those places] start to have access, [they'll] feel like it's homegrown. I think that's pretty cool."

–

Into a Brave New World

WORDS
Alexandra Svokos

PHOTOGRAPHS
Jacob Santiago

Fabrizio Cavallacci was 15 years old when he took over Caffe Reggio on MacDougal Street in the 1970s after the death of his mother. He "had several enemies around."

"They wanted to threaten me to leave the cafe," he said. But at one point, he said, "I know that they"—a different "they"—"spoke up for me."

"I've always been honest with them, and I never asked them anything, because once you ask them something, then they hook you up. That's no good. But I was always straightforward," he said. In return, he said, "the boys on Sullivan Street" were always straightforward with him in return.

"And when I say 'the boys,' I mean the mafia."

Sitting in the cafe at a table covered in bills and documents one hot, early summer day, Cavallacci was happy to tell me more. As I shuffled in the seat, my thighs sticking to the wooden chair in the heat, he sat assuredly in a full suit, with an American flag pin attached to the lapel of his navy jacket, eating an avocado salad and talking about his early days at Caffe Reggio, all while closely monitoring each person who walked in and placed an order.

His mother—a German woman, "not the type of woman that wanted to stay home"—asked his father to buy the cafe for her to run in 1955, and it has remained in the family since. His mother was quick to adapt to life in America, picking up English effortlessly. His father, though, born in Tuscany, only spoke Italian. He had a marble business in Queens, and everyone in that industry was Italian, so he had no need to learn English after they moved to America. After Cavallacci's mother died, the obvious successor to run the cafe was young Fabrizio: although born in Italy, he spoke English, had Social Security, and an American passport.

Fabrizio Cavallacci

ALLEVA
EST. 1892
ALLEVA
EST. 1892
MULBERRY ST
GRAND ST
ONE WAY
ONE WAY
ALLEVA
Ricotta
Mozzarella
Est. 1892
GELATO KING
HOME MADE GELATO & ITALIAN ICES
GELATO KING
ONE WAY

At the start, "the boys" made Cavallacci pay them every week—but at an amount that allowed him to still run the business, which wasn't that hard back in the mid 20th century when profit margins were much higher than today. "They were pretty honest. I'm not saying that they were dishonest," he said.

Eventually, they stopped asking for money, because they had found a new revenue stream.

"The toilet had a dime machine. Whoever wanted to use the toilet had to put 10 cents in... We were at a 50% cut with the boys," Cavallacci said, estimating the toilet made $800 a month. "And we had a cigarette machine, which used to belong to the boys. Obviously, they used to put [in] cigarettes not from New York state, but from Virginia, where they used to cost a lot less."

It was all good business, he said. In those days, even the city health inspectors were corrupt, so what could you say about some boys who just wanted a little cut of cash in return for "protection" whenever fishermen from the West Village docks would get into fights on the street outside and break the cafe's windows?

"But if someone would not want to pay, well, they would be in trouble," Cavallacci said. "For instance, Caffe Dante—they didn't want to pay, so one week, he got his windows broken. Another week, he got robbed. And still he didn't want to pay. So, see [that] old machine, the old espresso machine? Well, they had something similar. Without those arms, you could not make the espresso. So, what did they do? The boys said, 'You don't want to pay, you're not going to be able to make coffee.' They unscrewed the arms from their machine and they could not function for weeks, because in those days, they didn't have spare parts. So then they came to their senses. They started paying and they got their parts back."

Italians came to New York City in masses in the decades after the 1890s, Kenneth T. Jackson, a retiring professor and preeminent expert on the city of New York, said. They became a huge portion of the city's population. Making a "gross generalization," he said Italians tended "to be more territorial" than other ethnic groups. And so they gathered in spaces like lower Manhattan, establishing the area now known as Little Italy. The neighborhood has shrunk considerably in the past few decades, as Italians left Manhattan as part of white flight in the 1980s.

My family witnessed this change. My grandparents moved from Italy to America with their kids in the 1960s, settling into an Italian community in Bay Ridge, in Brooklyn. My grandparents knew 10 words of English between them when they arrived, and they'd drive into Little Italy in Manhattan to have dinner or get Italian specialties at the grocery stores there. By the 1990s, the crew had all left for the suburbs, where a massive Italian-American community continues to exist.

Little Italy, Jackson said, "seems to the outsider" like a unified group of Italians living together. But here's another "generalization," he said: "and in that sense, it's true of almost all immigrant groups: it's only outsiders who see it as a stable neighborhood." Inside, there is a "churning," Jackson described it, as the immigrants saw themselves not as Italians, which itself was just barely a unified nation, but as members of different regions.

"They thought of themselves as being from this place or that place [in Italy]," but Americans thought of them derogatorily as all the same. So, Jackson said, "They began to forge an Italian identity." It was that unity against discrimination that made "the boys" more acceptable, according to Cavallacci.

"Mafia grew up in New York as [an organization that wanted to] defend the Italian person that's over here," he said. "You know, 'If they do something wrong to you, you come to us, and we'll take care of it.'"

This is different from the mafia my family knows. Where my family comes from in Italy, you get hushed if you mention it. Your nonna might declare "there's no such thing as the mafia." But then someone will mention an uncle you've never heard of, and when you ask who he is, you're told: "the prosecutor who was executed in his office in the '80s."

With that in mind, I asked Cavallacci if he was comfortable casually telling me stories about his dealings with the mob, in broad—and socially distanced—daylight. He didn't seem too bothered by it. For one thing, he said that what happened was in the past—thanks to the then-district attorney by the name of Giuliani, who went after them. For another thing, this was really about the cohesion of the Italian community.

Despite this, there's a certain sense of shame the mafia brings to some Italian Americans—the National Italian American Foundation would sure like to bury the tales in the Meadowlands marshes, calling mafia movies degrading, built on stereotypes outside of reality for most Italian Americans.

And yet.

"Dante's did have a reputation," where you'd find "tough guys" drinking coffee outside, said journalist Jacob Margolies. It was a mixed crowd of people at the MacDougal street cafe, he said, and they were "part of the milieu, which kind of made it more interesting."

Margolies wrote an article for Amherst College's "The Common" about seeing a man his dad called "Sammy the Rat" at Caffe Dante in 1978. He said the cafe—which was opened in 1915 and owned by Italians for a 100 years before being taken over by Australians, who turned it into a trendy cocktail bar simply called Dante's—was a perfect place to spend a few hours with a friend or a book.

"And with your book, you might overhear Sammy the Rat talking about throwing someone off the roof of the building down the block, or a man and woman having a conversation about their relationship, or someone having an affair, whatever it was. It was kind of entertaining—more than entertaining, it was interesting. It was meaningful, or it could be," he said.

Given the real violence these people had brought to New York City, what could make stories about the mafia meaningful? The thought of danger dressed in a nice suit might be electrifying, but it might not seem entirely meaningful.

But no matter your feelings on them—and yes, they were (and, to an extent, are) violent, power-hungry, and so on—the New York mob are a meaningful part of the overall story of Italians trying to find their way in a city that could be rude and cold, just as they were working to learn what it meant to be Italian in a new country. As immigrants, they might still see themselves as members of different regions, but they recognize the need to look out for each other, to be there for each other, as they built a new community.

Mafia stories help paint a picture of this community growth within Manhattan, but it takes all the other stories—including the endless tales of small moments that maybe aren't quite as titillating—to really see it.

So here's one story I heard while reporting on this piece: One day, Professor Jackson wandered into Rao's, the famed Italian restaurant in Harlem dating back to 1896, without a reservation. They acted, he said, like "[I had] lost my mind"—"like it was clearly absurd" to think he could get in without a reservation.

"I thought I was Mr. New York, you know, teaching New York for all this time, edited the "Encyclopedia of New York City," president of the New York Historical Society—fat lot of difference that made," he laughed.

And here's another story I heard, when I told my nonna I was writing this article: One New Year's Eve, when my mom and her siblings were teenagers and all had plans with their friends, my grandparents found themselves alone with nothing to do. They decided to drive into the city from Brooklyn to celebrate New Year's Eve at their favorite restaurant in Little Italy—she can't remember the name now.

They didn't call ahead. They didn't have a reservation. The place was packed, of course. The owner saw them standing in the doorway and greeted them with kisses. Then he went into a back room, pulled out a table, and set it up, just for them.

–

Da Gennaro
Ristorante Italiano
Seafood
RISTORANTE
Da Gennaro
Brunch
Da Gennaro
CAFFE
DANTE
EST. 1915
CAFFE
DANTE
CAFFE
DANTE

Escaping the Grid

WORDS
Duncan Nielsen

PHOTOGRAPHS
Daniela Velasco

Manhattanites aren't going out of their way to find coffee. But if they're headed to a park, they won't need to: Adorning the edges of the city's public spaces are a host of purveyors offering perfectly coiffed milk and bean, available to those seeking respite from the city's tangle of hard right angles. The option to escape to a green space, however, didn't always exist.

At the turn of the 19th century, Manhattan was doomed to become a dense sheet of graph paper. Its population had doubled to 60,000 in the span of 10 years, prompting the city to develop the rolling hills, marshes, and farmlands that lay between Houston and 155th Street. They hired John Randel Jr., a surveyor with a fondness for booze and plenty of pluck, who leveled hills and ousted farmers as he meticulously forged the unending grid of the city that we know today.

But the Commissioners' Plan of 1811, as it's known, did little to accommodate the nature lover. American novelist Edith Wharton decried it upon proposal: "Rectangular New York," she began, "this cramped horizontal gridiron of a town without towers, porticoes, fountains, or perspectives, hide-bound in its deadly uniformity of mean ugliness." To her credit, not so much as a single square of green space had been reserved by Randel for public use.

As the population of New York continued to balloon through the early 1800s, an odd outdoors culture would take shape. Since not everyone could easily "go to the rivers for a breath of fresh air," as Randel retorted to Wharton, they instead took their families to picnic in alternative spaces, like nearby cemeteries. Those circumstances—but also a desire by New York's upper echelon to rival the pomp and circumstance of London and Paris—spurred the beginnings of Manhattan's first green space in 1853, Central Park.

MetLife

Smack-dab in the middle of the grid, a workforce of 200,000 immigrants planted 270,000 trees and shrubs, pushed and pulled six million cubic feet of dirt to form hills, plazas, and sunken roadways, and reformed rock with explosives to create the illusion that you'd been jettisoned out of the "mean ugliness." In present day, and to the benefit of the modern public, beautifully pulled espresso, cold brews, and specialty coffees now complement a foray into that vast green space that's continued to evolve over centuries.

It's important to note that Central Park has a murky history of classism and displacement (Seneca Village deserves volumes, and is worth an internet search), but Teranga Cafe in East Harlem, founded in 2018, is imbuing a unique culture back into the fold. "We created Teranga to bring Western African food to a wider audience," says co-founder Noah Levine, who explains the cafe's core ethos. "The word 'Teranga,' from the Wolofs in Senegal, is the concept of how you treat a stranger," he says. "Do you invite them to have a meal?"

Teranga's menu represents a holistic journey through the western part of the African continent, but Levine recommends a plate of chef Pierre Tham's Senegalese chicken yassa, rice pilaf, and of course, a single-origin Ethiopian cold brew. The coffee, and all of the cafe's ingredients—like watermelon, okra, and black-eyed peas—are sourced from small farmers in Western Africa. Local artists from the region produce typographies, symbols, and imagery that have been transcribed into the cafe's space. In pandemic-era New York, Teranga is providing artisanal blankets to park-goers looking to get outside.

Down the border of the park in the Upper East Side is Bluestone Lane, an Aussie-style cafe born of the cramped cobblestone alleys of Melbourne. In the '80s, Melbourne eased taxes to bring commerce back to its urban center. Speakeasy cafes pulling flat whites, long blacks, and everything in between soon flanked pubs on every street. Artisan coffee was a booming back-alley secret.

Bluestone Lane's owner and founder Nick Stone has since spilled the beans in New York. The small batch roaster's first two locations, established in 2013, were stuffed into the grid's crevices to follow Melbourne's word-of-mouth tradition. Today, one of its more remarkable locations is inside the vestibule of a church, and offers views of the Central Park pond that are nothing short of heavenly. If you ask its vice president, Nick's brother Andrew Stone, what to order for takeaway, he'll tell you: "Ah mate, it's gotta be a flat white and avocado smash toast!"

It's possible that no one in Manhattan has considered the grid's flow of foot traffic more than Claire and Chris Saphire, the wife-and-husband duo behind Little Bean on the northern side of Central Park. "If you don't pick a corner where people pass to catch the train, they're going to go somewhere else," says Chris, who, when deciding on a space to rent, camped out on different corners to count pedestrians walking by. Coming from a laid-back Los Angeles coffee culture, they found the pace was different, too. "If someone says light and sweet, you have to know what that means," says Chris. "Otherwise they're gonna be on to the next spot."

With Central Park a frisbee toss away, and the 2 and 3 lines just out front, commuters, tourists, and weekend warriors alike file in for a well-rounded menu. The award-winning, single-origin cold brew, however, is the thing to get. If iced beverages just aren't your bag, Chris says to keep an eye out for seasonal concoctions, like a lavender latte infused with organic syrup.

Far north of the hubbub of the city's center—and beyond the grips of John Randel Jr.'s manifest destiny—is Kuro Kirin, a viby locals' cafe in what The New York Times calls "the last affordable neighborhood in Manhattan." Even if gentrification comes knocking, Inwood, rich with untamed forests and rivers, is home to The Met Cloisters and Inwood Hill Park, and remains an oasis amid the cacophony of New York.

"When we were looking for a place to put our cafe, we fell in love with the outdoor spaces," recalls Dennis Blake, one of the seven partners of Kuro Kirin's coffee collective. Established in 2018, six years after sister cafe Kuro Kuma opened its doors, the cafes' strengths lie in their Japanese cold brew, steady-handed pulls of Counter Culture beans, and an ability to keep things simple. "Get a macchiato, cortado, cappuccino, or latte, straight up," says Dennis. "We just want to give you the highest quality that we can while taking away any perceived pretentiousness." Beyond the grip of the pressurized gridiron, amid ample greenery on an island otherwise latticed with cement and steel, it may just be worth going out of your way.

–

The Diner Is Whatever You Need It To Be

WORDS
Tess Falotico LaFaye

PHOTOGRAPHS
Daniela Velasco

When the bar is closing and only mozzarella sticks will do, the diner is an after-party. On Sunday morning, as a veteran waiter delivers greasy homefries and tops up sturdy, ceramic mugs of hot coffee, the diner is a hangover cure. When there's time to kill and nowhere to go, the diner is home base. Sitting bleary-eyed at the counter, pouring half-and-half from a stainless-steel creamer into black coffee, the diner is a fuel-up. After the little league game or the dance recital or the track meet, the diner is a victory lap or a consolation prize. A great diner is whatever you need it to be.

Diners as we know them evolved from the mobile lunch wagons, or "dining cars," that powered workers in the late 19th century. As cars became ubiquitous, the need (and street space) for these self-contained, moving restaurants waned. Opportunistic manufacturers like Patrick Tierney, who is often credited with shortening the term "dining car" to "diner," pivoted by selling their prefab restaurants and shipping them, booths and all, to become stationary establishments, some of which still stand in Manhattan today. In 1946, Empire Diner was shipped from the Fodero Dining Car Company to 10th Avenue; its chrome shell and iconic sign remain, but it has been turned over many times, becoming more polished with each new owner. In the same decade, the Pullman Dining Car Co. manufactured the Square Diner in New Jersey and sent it to the city, where it still sits on the corner of Leonard and Varick in TriBeCa.

While Manhattan has lost many classic spots to rent hikes and rapid commercial development (R.I.P., Cup & Saucer), some have remained wonderfully, almost stubbornly, intact. Pearl Diner, opened in the 1960s, survives in its original single-story building among the towers of the Financial District— you can still sit at the formica counter and watch the cooks work the griddle. It is one of only four stand-alone diners that remain in Manhattan. Similarly, Tom's Restaurant, near Columbia University, has been in the same family since it opened in the 1940, even

PEARL
DINER
DINER
EXIT

PEARL
DINER
NO PARKING ANYTIME
NO STANDING ANYTIME

PEARL
D

Golden Diner

Samuel Yoo

NO FACE MASK
NO ENTRY

after becoming a magnet for "Seinfeld" fans when its facade appeared in nearly every episode of the show.

On some menus, reliable diner staples—turkey clubs, pancakes, milkshakes—sit alongside more distinctive comfort foods. At Eisenberg's Sandwich Shop, that's eggy, fried matzo brei. Traditionally served only at Passover, the dish is available year-round at the 91-year-old Flatiron restaurant. Odessa, a hold-out of the East Village's shrinking "Little Ukraine," serves eggs-any-style with sides like kielbasa, as well as pierogi and blintzes.

Golden Diner is the rare newcomer that retains the unpretentiousness and accessibility of the diner genre while looking at it with a fresh perspective. For example, here, the fan-favorite is a club sandwich made with crispy chicken katsu. Samuel Yoo grew up eating at old-school diners in Queens before working in the Major Food Group and Momofuku restaurant groups and ultimately opening his own diner in 2019. Yoo worked with Kopi Trading Company, which specializes in sourcing Asian beans, to custom-roast Golden Diner's coffee beans. His goal was to achieve a more nuanced (read: less burnt) version of the robust diner coffee he grew up with, and to source the best-quality beans he could while still offering free refills.

Another new-ish, albeit more stylized, standout is four-year-old Metrograph Commissary, just a few blocks away on Ludlow Street, which serves thoughtful, seasonal, satisfying food all day—a gem lettuce Caesar salad, a turkey club with caciocavallo, steak frites. Baristas pull shots of espresso for cortados and flat whites and brew pour-over coffee from various George Howell-roasted beans. Attached to an art-house movie theater of the same name, Metrograph is a workhorse, the kind of place where you can go for fried eggs and potatoes in the morning, a glass of wine before dinner, or a burger at 1 a.m. That is, after all, what a great diner is: a utility restaurant, serving many purposes for many people, often at the same time. No matter what you need, no matter what time it is, and no matter how much the city changes, the diner always has a seat for you.

–

Coffee in the Time of Corona

Words
Brian Aubrey Smith

PHOTOGRAPHS
Atticus Radley

Black Fox Coffee's flagship in the Financial District of New York City sits just off the corner of Pine and Pearl, and its understated storefront on the first floor of the 67-story building at 70 Pine blends well with the block. It's easy to miss if you're not part of its crowd of quick-paced regulars working in the neighborhood's office towers.

When asked what he'd missed most about his day-to-day behind the counter at Black Fox Coffee, Jonathan Wilson said, "I missed being busy. It's a very busy coffee shop on a good day, and we have lots of good days during the week. One of my favorite things was being in the thick of it when it was a little rushed. It worked a different part of your head and it's been frustrating not being able to get back to that."

Wilson was speaking in early July 2020, six months into the COVID-19 pandemic caused by the virus SARS-CoV-2. New York's shutdown, introduced in March, has been especially difficult for small businesses like coffee shops that have seen their business and day-to-day operations mutate several times.

Variety Roasters, which has grown to five stores in New York since its inception in 2008, has quieter cafes sprinkled across Manhattan and Brooklyn. Owner Gavin Compton lamented, "That time to catch up with each individual person is totally gone now when you're wearing a mask and you can only have one person in the store at a time. It makes it way more awkward."

Across stores and across neighborhoods, the COVID-19 pandemic has flipped normal dynamics on their head, then flipped them again. It has warped the way coffee shop owners, regulars, and employees interact with one another and the physical spaces of their shops, cafes, coffee bars, and sidewalks.

Each shop has seen its own distinct set of changes in customer base and mood. Black Fox Coffee, for example, has transformed from a

COFFEE

BLACK
FOX
COFFEE CO.
WE ARE OPEN!
8AM - 4PM DAILY
Order in-store or ahead via our website
or by downloading our App.
blackfoxcoffee.com

Daniel Murphy & Sarah Appleby Murphy

COFFEE

GOOD LUCK
OUT THERE

Jonathan Wilson

bustling, thousand-cup-a-day downtown terminal to a more tranquil, neighborhood drop-in.

"During [this pandemic], it's been 95% residents, but in a normal world we're seeing about 75% daily workers in the area and the remaining 25% is a mix of tourists and residents," said owner Daniel Murphy. Ground Support in SoHo has seen its weekend traffic change from 80% tourist to 99% regular, and it has picked up new regulars from the already close-knit neighborhood along the way.

"During these times, it's [about] 99% [regulars]," said founder Steven Sadof. "We've had some times where, whether it's been during [the pandemic] or after the [Black Lives Matter] protests, that people wanted to come to SoHo and see what the devastation was like. Ninety-nine percent of people who are coming in are our friends, who are within walking distance, because people aren't riding the subway."

Even curious visitors checking out the empty SoHo streets or the shattered glass and boarded up windows after nights of unrest might be reminded to be respectful of the neighborhood and its residents, said Sadof.

What hasn't changed in the four months of lockdown is that shop owners and employees miss the pre-pandemic rituals of their shops. But they're looking for silver linings in these new interpersonal dynamics.

To a person, owners and workers at stores that had previously become accustomed to high-volume traffic have enjoyed the change of pace, and the space and time it has afforded them.

"It's that very small-town feel now," said Sadof of Ground Support, an iconic independent operation that's always been very neighborhood-forward.

"Ultimately, it's been a pretty rewarding experience. We've seen the same people come in at the same time every day for the past three months," he said. "Despite the sort of closeness and warmth that SoHo had before, it has become so much tighter. The pace of business has slowed down. The pace of life slowed down because nobody really had anywhere to go. Neighbors were all talking to each other and talking to us. It really felt like a small town for the past three months, which was wonderful and a great distraction or comfort in otherwise difficult times."

Murphy of Black Fox noticed an even more dramatic shift. "We're such a busy, high-volume cafe that being able to slow down and have a lingering conversation with our customers and ask them a few more questions about their day that we wouldn't be able to do when [there are] six people in line behind them," he said. "So just slowing it all down and having more time to spend one-on-one with our customers has been great."

Some more spacious cafes, like Variety Roasters, weren't built on heavy morning or commuter traffic. But even it has found ways to appreciate a slower pace.

Ciera Torres—a New York City native, ten-year veteran of the city's coffee scene, and manager of Variety Roasters' Williamsburg location since February—noted that, "From a behind the counter standpoint, one nice thing is that... people are paying more attention. They're asking more questions about our coffee."

"We're also able to understand how people want their coffee fixed," she said. Instead of serving them a "cup with room," she's been able to understand how regular customers prefer their coffee and to make it for them.

VARIETY
COFFEE
Great Taste

261
COFFEE
COFFEE
VARIETY
ROASTERS

COFFEE
VARIETY
ROASTERS
13
LUCKY SHOT
ESPRESSO
6
LUCKY SHOT
ESPRESSO
Dutch Cocoa, Molasses, Fig Jam
10
27
LUCKY SHOT
ESPRESSO
Honeycomb, Melon, Key Lime Pie
30
3

Curran Boyd

buybuy
BABY
Coffee Brewer
Cafetière
CHEMEX
VARIETY

That they're able to find silver linings doesn't mean that shop owners aren't itching for a return to normal, especially those whose businesses and cultures were reliant on the ability for customers to linger.

As much as the pandemic has demanded resiliency and fostered a deeper connection with regular customers, it's come at the expense of comfort in a New York that, already rushed and unforgiving, has somehow managed to become more anxious.

"Customers are missing the option to linger," said Compton of Variety Roasters. "We've stayed open and the menu hasn't really changed, but everything we're doing now is a little rushed and a little less comfortable and a little inhibited. People being able to run into a friend in a cafe and linger over a conversation is something that is missing."

At Black Fox Coffee, it's the energy that's missing, said Steven Levy, Head of Operations. "In New York, whether it's for the good or the bad, everyone becomes accustomed to the hustle and bustle, and how crazy it is. Even though at times you kind of hate it, it's something that, because you get so used to it, it's definitely feeling like it's missing at the moment."

It has also come at the expense of employees. Ground Support cut hours and staff drastically. Black Fox Coffee is down to six employees from 36. At one point Variety Roaster's team shrunk from 55 members to nine.

"[At Ground Support] we had to let almost everybody go. The solution to that is to get behind the counter," said Sadof.

"[I'm most looking forward to] getting our team back together," said Murphy from Black Fox Coffee. We had such a great team [before the pandemic] and we had such great talent across all disciplines—back of house, front of house, our baristas, our coffee director. So just getting that team back together and the rapport back and seeing everyone functioning at a really high level is something I'm really looking forward to."

For Wilson, speaking from behind his counter in the Financial District, the change is something to look forward to.

"It feels entirely different now. It's kind of uncharted territory moving forward. A lot of the systems and habits that we had in place are no longer applicable. It's kind of like starting over a little bit, and that will be really exciting," he said.

As she wrapped up the day, Torres thought of a return to normal almost celebratorily. "I feel like I took it for granted a little bit before. You're thinking, 'It's always so busy, it's always so packed.' You can kind of see all the bad in it," she said.

"But you know when your grandmother's cooking in the kitchen and everyone comes in and takes a bite? That's how I always felt about the cafe. Everyone is entering my kitchen for a moment and hanging out. I miss having that space to let people take a moment."

–

Weekday Warriors

WORDS
Dale Arden Chong

PHOTOGRAPHS
Adam Goldberg, Daniela Velasco

Strip away the people, taxi cabs, and buildings, along with everything else that makes up the surface layers of New York City, and you'll find that the structural bones of one of the largest cultural hubs in the world all connect through one borough: Manhattan. If Manhattan is considered the heart of New York City, and the people who work and reside in it its blood, the city's 15 trains lines and 21 bridges are the vessels that keep everything moving smoothly without skipping a beat.

Spanning the East River is the Brooklyn Bridge, which has become one of the city's most iconic landmarks to date. Complete with granite towers and steel cables, the John Augustus Roebling design officially opened in 1883, providing commuters a safe option to move between Manhattan and Brooklyn by foot, bicycle, car, and other modes of transportation for the first time.

On the other side of the island, crossing the New York-New Jersey state line is the Holland Tunnel. New York's first vehicle pathway under the Hudson River, it opened in 1927 as the first mechanically ventilated underwater tunnel, eventually earning the title of a National Historic Landmark in 1993, according to The Port Authority of New York and New Jersey.

Manhattan's bridges and tunnels hallmark some of the most notable architectural achievements in U.S. history, ultimately becoming a pillar of New York culture. Like its coffee culture, New York wouldn't be the same without its mass transit systems. At some stations, like the Financial District's Fulton subway stop—which runs the A, C, E, 1, 2, and 3 lines and houses Voyager Espresso—Manhattan's transportation and coffee cultures meet. However, it's the commuters, who rely on both during the work week, that make traveling to and from the city a quintessentially New York routine.

"I'm addicted to coffee," said Kelsey Weekman, a writer at In The Know, a Verizon Media website that covers the latest news in tech, gaming,

LIGHT

PETROSSIAN
ONE WAY

style, and more. The Fort Greene, Brooklyn resident commutes daily on the R train from Delkab to the 8th Street/NYU subway stop before grabbing her coffee from City of Saints or The Bean and heading to her office in the East Village. "I always pick it up after I get off the train so I can let my brain be mush for a few extra moments and keep one hand on the railing and the other on my phone."

While some like Weekman make a point to pick up coffee at a shop, Alexis Diaz prefers to make her coffee at home in Hasbrook Heights. The New Jersey native's path to Manhattan takes her through the Lincoln Tunnel and drops her off at Port Authority. Diaz, who was working in Condé Nast's Style Division as a sales assistant before the COVID-19 quarantine, sees coffee as something special for herself. "When I was in school, I'd take it with me in a canteen…it was a treat for enduring another bus ride and prep for another long day," she said. "At Condé [Nast], the coffee was complimentary, so my daily cup was a moment to pause and appreciate being part of a company I always admired."

Of course, for part of a day that's so routine, it's understandable if the people serving the coffee become just as important as the drink itself—and for Michelle Cobham, a man she knows only as Carlos became family. "I started going to Carlos when I first moved to Queens. He had a cart right outside our train station," she shared. The Director and Human Resource Business Partner at Macy's—who takes the E train to Penn Station—explained how she would always get a small coffee from Carlos each morning, as well as a hot chocolate and a pastry for her daughter. "Over the years we formed a relationship; we often talked about our kids, family, and life. He had become a fixture in our lives." However, Carlos suffered from a stroke, losing the vibrancy Cobham was so used to. A few months later, he passed away. "That was actually the last time I ever bought coffee from an NYC coffee cart." Now, she gets her coffee from Starbucks at the train station before heading straight to the office.

Daily commutes may seem mundane on the surface. However, the minutes spent on the train, bus, or even the sidewalk begin to add up. And before you know it, they, just like coffee, become one of the most crucial parts of Manhattan life.

–

Felix Roasting Co.

A Mindful Cup

WORDS
Georgie Carroll

PHOTOGRAPHS
Adam Goldberg, Daniela Velasco

"To 'coffee' is to connect with friends, exchange ideas, create, or structure one's day," says Claire Chan, ex-fashion buyer and owner of West Village cafe The Elk.

Coffee has fueled conversation in New York City since its advent. Since migrant Jewish intelligentsia and artists sought out coffeehouses at the end of the nineteenth century, they have been spaces for thinking and rethinking. Coffeehouses remain connected to freedom of thought and dialogue. In a culturally rich, constantly changing place like Manhattan, a cup of joe has come to defy rather than represent any kind of norm. Coffee is consistently redefined and repositioned. Maybe that's why independent cafes remain so close to cultural movements, as spaces in which to reimagine, to break away.

Women and coffee in the city go back over 100 years. New York businesswoman Alice MacDougall opened The Little Coffee House in Grand Central Station in 1919, capturing the female imagination. Women had previously been forbidden from public eateries and colonial coffeehouses, as places for males to discuss business and politics. MacDougall's cafes sprung up around Manhattan, odes to a European aesthetic with stone-clad interiors, the fountains and Roman-style columns of Firenze (West 46th Street) and the theatrical Spanish patio of Sevilla (West 57th Street). She published books on her signature dish "Coffee and Waffles" (1926), as well as "Autobiography of a Business Woman" two years later. According to Erin Meister's "New York City Coffee: A Caffeinated History" (2017) "She was a true character, a true New Yorker and an absolute individual." Her business didn't survive the Depression but her legacy of connecting coffee with female voices reverberates in the city today.

Coffee is still a male-dominated industry. But recent years have seen many more women working in production, roasting, training, and hospitality. Malaysia-born barista Chi-Sum Ngai and her partner

Kaleena Teoh opened Coffee Project NY in the East Village in 2015. It became famous for its deconstructed latte. They now teach certified classes to coffee industry professionals. The Perch, at the stylish women's co-working space The Wing in SoHo, is run by highly skilled, female coffee connoisseurs, and is dedicated to supporting women working in the industry. A high volume of Q-Graders (certified coffee connoisseurs) are women, as is the case among the staff and board members of the certifying Coffee Quality Institute. Q-Grader Erika Vonie won the highly competitive New York Coffee Masters competition in 2017 before starting her e-commerce business Trade, located in Manhattan. She provides consultancy services too, from barista training to brand imaging.

The story around coffee is also changing. Fusion cafes selling healthy, organic, and vegan foods along with natural lifestyle and beauty products increasingly associate coffee with wellness. At The Elk, you can enjoy a "cinn-full latte" alongside a seasonal rice bowl, for example. At its general store you can buy palo santo, soy candles, and dried as well as fresh flowers, products that denote rituals. And by being associated with popular products like these, coffee becomes incorporated into experiences of wellness, and even "consumer spirituality," which is concerned with finding meaning, self-reflection, the inner state, and inner self. Coffee forms more of a ritual than ever, a moment to pause rather than to press on.

The Elk is slick, clean, and confident. In its own way it reflects the importance of clarity, calm, and connection. "It's more than a beverage," says Chan, who has noticed how the emphasis on wellness, which attracts a predominantly female clientele, has seen a change in coffee culture.

"We take great pride in the fact that we are female-owned and managed," she says. The Elk is a minority, female-founded small business with a majority BIPOC team. It cares about supporting female and minority-brands. "I am fortunate enough to work with many talented and inspiring women," says Chan. "The culture is one of care, empathy, and attention to detail." If coffee is about conversation, then meeting places like The Elk emphasize the importance of listening. "I believe our clientele reacts to this and we react to them—it is a back and forth. This has created a certain warmth and sensitivity within our community at large."

On owning a coffee business as a woman she says, "Your femininity is your greatest strength. It shapes your point of view, and having a unique point of view in this industry is everything."

Coffee is becoming more responsible—more ethical, less throw-away. Some businesses are associating it with a consumer desire to reconnect to nature. The PlantShed, owned by the Mourkakos family, whose roots in the New York floral business date to the Great Depression, has added a cafe to support business. The addition of coffee encourages in-person shopping that fosters community. Coffee becomes a surprising antidote to the alienation of urban living. Remi Flower and Coffee serves visually unique coffees—with violet—or crimson-colored creams, topped with lavender or rose petals. As well as making highly shareable drinks, Remi is also reclaiming the coffee break through a hyper-feminine aesthetic.

As coffee culture moves into the wellness space, the celebratory trend of the feminine soul and spirit is being incorporated into the aesthetics of some coffee brands. Matt Moinian of Felix Roasting Co. recognizes that "specialty coffee houses have often fallen into a hyper-masculine culture and aesthetic, which can be quite alienating." The flagship of his coffee company on Park Avenue South has been described as a "sumptuous coffee sanctuary" by Vogue. The Ken Fulk design team and the team at Felix Roasting Co. worked with strong female leads to create the space. Its geometric patterns, with a dusty-pink, copper, and teal palette; cues

Josh Richmond

 Reagan Petrehn

Reagan Petrehn

to a locomotive aesthetic, with railway dining-car-style seating; and bistro detailing with classical accents speak to a heritage that seems to echo MacDougall's Old World-style cafes.

A 'coffee sanctuary' would not long ago have sounded like an oxymoron in a city like New York. Felix Roasting Co. associates its product with mental calm, even mindfulness, inviting customers to "take an extra minute to consider their daily routine." Enjoying a cup of coffee at Felix, Moinian says, is "an act of self-care."

"We decided it was going to be sacred ground," Moinian tells me, describing the central bar area known as The Sanctuary. "We don't take ourselves too seriously, but the exact point where we prepare our coffee and hand it over is the culmination of a lot of hard work, and we do care about that moment." The space features a copper dome over the bar and "sacred geometry," as Moinian describes it, on the ceiling, inspired by the Vatican. Three female figures painted onto tiles watch over the team as "a reminder of the attributes we value as a brand"—they represent Passion, Dedication, and Authenticity.

Coffee and divine feminine imagery is well-known to us from perhaps the most recognizable coffee logo in the world. Starbucks, which opened its first store in Manhattan on the Upper West Side, has a logo so familiar we barely notice it now. The twinned-tailed mermaid is infused with pre-Christian symbolism. She is, ultimately, The Great Mother, related to the wisdom of the deep and the regenerative quality of water. This siren-like creature descends from the serpent, which is often depicted with stars, and other mystical imagery, from crescent moons to horns, connecting her with light, creation, and the egg.

The tiled mural at Felix Roasting Co. includes a tree of life, from which springs creativity. It symbolizes "the various efforts and people involved in making Felix a success... Our muses tend to and worship the tree, cultivating its growth and in turn feed and protect all who come."

Maybe it's because Felix Roasting Co. is so passionate about the source of its coffee that female creative energy became a channel for the aesthetic. The brand is meticulous, carrying its dedication to quality and innovation from origin to cup. Besides oat and nut milks, Felix makes its own tonic water and marshmallows. A look at the website reveals something like a hymn to nature: to the harvests, seasons, soil, climate, sunlight, the stories of the producers: "It is in everything that we do."

The company ethos is laid out in a booklet called the "Culture Almanac," pictured on the website amongst other collateral. The title feels relevant, with a growing awareness of natural cycles and rhythms in the air. Across gender, these have become more of a mainstream way of thinking about productivity, with ultradian rhythms, for example, now a part of commercial vocabulary.

As well as innovating coffee through its menus, Felix Roasting Co. feels like a beautifully packaged coffee Renaissance. The brand seems to epitomize the change in coffee culture that is taking place across the city. Coffee is lingering, conscious, deep, and opens up limitless possibilities. The feminine energy seems to have sprung itself on them as much as it has been drawn into the design. It's an energy that is already working a power of its own all over the city, impressing and insisting on more conscious ways of working and living. All of life happens under the goddesses' watchful eyes—"Businesses have started at our tables, films have been written, breakups, first dates, family reunions, you name it," Moinian says.

Coffee belongs to everybody. It's a drink that starts the day, punctuates it, sets a tone for it, keeps it going. It still fuels the workforce, as it has always done. It's still feeding conversations. It just seems to be doing it with a very valuable, very sustainable, new sort of wisdom.

–

Over Drinks

WORDS
Dale Arden Chong

PHOTOGRAPHS
Daniela Velasco

It's hard to imagine New York City without thinking about its nightlife. After all, it has been dubbed "The City That Never Sleeps." There are an infinite number of reasons why someone may choose to pack up their bags and move to the bustling city. But it might be this unofficial title, along with the allure of New York's day-to-night-to-day lifestyle, that draws transplants from across the country and around the globe—and more specifically, its most populated borough, Manhattan. But with a reputation and a state of mind focused on movement around the clock, it begs the question, what keeps New York awake?

In the fast-moving lines pouring out of neighborhood joints and queued up at unassuming stands on the sidewalk—which are complete with the city's iconic "We Are Happy To Serve You" to-go cups—it's as clear as day: New York runs on coffee. And whether it's meant to fuel the long hours of a workday or accompany a Saturday morning brunch, this caffeinated drink feels as familiar to the city and all its residents as walking. But once the sun dips below Manhattan's skyline and the city lights sparkle against the concrete jungle, the hum of New York begins singing a different tune. Coffee is no longer New York's nectar—instead, it's another Manhattan staple: alcohol.

Like its caffeinated counterpart, alcohol is embedded into Manhattan's lifestyle. According to Giles Russell, the co-founder of Two Hands—which has locations in TriBeCa, NoHo, Nolita, and Williamsburg—both beverages are a natural fit for the borough. "New Yorkers are incredibly social beings. You don't want to live in a city that is literally packed to the gills with people and not want to see and talk with others," he shared. "Coffee and alcohol are both social lubricants; they are the two starting points for any social interaction—'Want to grab coffee?' and 'Let's grab a drink together.' It makes so much sense that Manhattanites are avid coffee and alcohol drinkers." Zachary Sharaga, the founder of Dear Mama in Harlem, shares the same sentiment and sees coffee and liquor as vessels to bring people together. "As much as

Bar Pisellino

coffee is considered fuel, I've always thought of alcohol as a similar fuel," he said. "Coffee and alcohol have fueled conversation, creativity, and community for a very long time."

Dear Mama homes in on cultivating a space where people can gather. By operating as both a cafe and a bar, Sharaga created a watering hole that co-exists with his customers' lives—whether it be throughout the day or at the milestones that shape each individual's journey. This emphasis on building dialogue among individuals has been a pillar for the company, even playing a part in its locations. "We chose to locate Dear Mama far away from a commercial district and on a side street to afford us the ability to have ample space for events and gatherings, and give people the flexibility to have meaningful conversations without the transactional feeling many coffee shops have…in a city like New York," he shared.

Anyone from the outside looking in would see the mood in Manhattan shift as soon as the workday ends. But according to both Russell and Sharaga, the transition is more fluid than that. For Russell, this shift simply reflects what Two Hands' patrons want. "Our guests think of us as an all-day spot. You can come to us and have a Bloody Mary at 8 a.m. or a cappuccino at 10 p.m., or vice versa," Russell said. "We are here for whatever our guests need when they walk in." Bar Pisellino, according to co-founder Jody Williams, also looks to give its community a full day-to-night experience, inspired by the Italian bar culture—something her partner Rita Sodi longed for. "[She] had been missing out on the Italian aperitivo and morning coffee experience since she left Florence," Williams said. Located across the street from their other restaurant Via Carota, Bar Pisellino has seamlessly found its place, like a new friend, among the West Village community. "[We are] dedicated to the art of drinking Italian style, starting with espresso culture and continuing with cocktails and aperitivi. This is a very traditional approach to Italian drinking, all captured in our little bar."

When the time comes to turn the attention away from things you *have* to think about to what you *want* to think about, Manhattan's cafes and bars are ready for the task. To set the tone for their patrons, these establishments reset their spaces to reflect a new phase of daily relationships by dimming the lights or changing the music. However, establishments like Felix Roasting Co. are also bringing the daytime experience into the night with its creative coffee cocktails. "Coffee and alcohol are both art forms and serve a need to the person imbibing them," founder Matt Moinian said. "I think there is a natural connection between the two, especially when done elegantly and as a craft."

Felix Roasting Co. aims to elevate the everyday routine of drinking coffee—be it through the interior design of its cafe or the drinks it serves. The brand also takes that approach with its cocktails, opting to use specific glassware to enhance different drinks on its menu. "We look for innovative ways to present coffee, bringing the natural characteristics to the forefront for the customer with a unique presentation."

While Felix Roasting Co. offers its customers memorable drinking experiences through innovative cocktails like its signature Felix Hickory Smoked Latte or the Deconstructed Espresso Tonic, the Financial District's Dead Rabbit puts its focus on perfecting the Irish Coffee. According to the bar's beverage director Jillian Vose, the bar's founders—Jack McGarry and Sean Muldoon—decided to include its take on the age-old classic on its menu to build a knowledge and appreciation for Irish whiskey. "It was and still is the most commonly known classic cocktail using Irish whiskey," she shared. "The problem was nobody, including ourselves, had ever really had a good one. We'd have to change people's minds on that one, too." The result? Dead Rabbit's most popular drink and staple—which is joined by two other cocktails featuring coffee, the Small Change and Irish Coffee Martini.

"Coffee is a [universally] known ingredient for guests. Everyone can relate to it," Vose explains as to why Dead Rabbit incorporates the drink into a selection of its cocktails. For its Irish Coffee specifically, Vose notes that coffee and whiskey complement each other flavor-wise. However, it also provides its consumer the unique sensation of a jolting pick-me-up while also mellowing them out simultaneously.

Perhaps this co-existence of coffee and alcohol describes the Manhattan social life perfectly. "They are inextricably linked as nectars from which people draw strength and calm as required," Moinian expressed. Plus, they each serve as catalysts to interact with each other over occasions like first dates, birthdays, and even business meetings. "New York is all energy, creativity, and culture. I think coffee and alcohol are the fuel that make that engine run."

Whether it's through a cup of coffee or something a little stronger, these establishments and the drinks they serve play a role in something bigger, something that transcends beyond the last call: the everyday experiences that define a person's life.

–

A Taste of Malaysia in Manhattan

WORDS
Faye Bradley

PHOTOGRAPHS
Adam Goldberg, Daniela Velasco

A cornerstone for Manhattan's Chinatown locals, Kopitiam pays tribute to the Malaysian traditional cafe by serving a selection of the best flavors and cuisine from the Malaysian peninsula. We spoke to co-owner, Moonlynne Tsai, on how Kopitiam and Malay culture has woven itself into Manhattan's coffee scene, and why she chose the eatery to be located in Chinatown.

A *kopi tiam* is a traditional coffee shop reflecting the polyglot heritage of Singaporean culture, where *"kopi"* means coffee in Malay and *"tiam"* translates to shop in Hokkien. Situated on the Lower East Side of Manhattan, Kopitiam serves *baba-nyonya* cuisine, a merger between the cuisines of Chinese immigrants and locals on the Malaysian peninsula. So this Lower East Side cafe's name, Kopitiam, conjures a coalescence of cultures and flavors which has developed over years of savoring the tradition of *kopi tiam* cafes from Singapore. Coffee at a *kopi tiam* is unlike what you'd find at Western cafes, which typically contain a high amount of caffeine—*kopi* is made from Robusta beans and the flavor is enhanced by wok-frying them with butter, lard, or sugar, then drip-brewing the grinds through a sock. The drink is served with teaspoons of sugar and sweetened condensed milk—which was a cheaper option back in the colonial era. At Kopitiam, the owners import exclusively roasted beans from Penang. Tsai explains how the coffee is served, "Our coffee is imported from Kung Kee Roastery in Penang, so our black coffee is roasted over charcoal with some sugar and margarine to give a robust butter flavor. Our white coffee is a take on the very popular instant coffees in Asia, usually called 3-in-1 (which typically feature coffee, creamer, and sugar already in the mix)."

Kopitiam—which was opened as a joint venture between chef Kyo Pang and restaurateur Moonlynn Tsai—aims to resemble the traditional coffee shop and honors the Pang family's Malaysian background and their family recipes. Pang and Tsai took a three-month backpacking trip around Southeast Asia, exploring Malaysia, Cambodia, and Thailand, before arriving in Penang, where Pang's grandfather lives. There, they

discovered more about the traditional *kopi tiam* and decided to bring those traditions to the United States. Their menu features traditional Malay dishes, including *otak-otak* fish quiche steamed in banana leaf and pork deep-fried in bean curd sheets. Both are reminiscent of Malaysia's rich and long-standing culinary culture.

Buzzing with activity (enhanced by its cult following on social media), Kopitiam is much more than a picture-perfect hotspot. Pang grew up in Malaysia where coffee shops are often ramshackle, multi-generational places where people go to read the morning paper and catch up with family and friends. Straddling Chinatown and the Lower East Side, Kopitiam recreates this family-centric atmosphere, as it attracts a range of people from different communities, from teenagers to the elderly. "The goal is to [reflect the] family lineage [and] culture [through] food, so the menu has a heavy emphasis on *nyonya* cuisine" says Tsai on Pang's previous business, which was a small, four-seater not far from Kopitiam.

At the moment, there are few *kopi tiams* in New York City, so Tsai and Pang were excited to share their version by opening their cafe. However, there is a growing community of Malaysians in the area who miss their homeland and culture. "There aren't many Malaysian businesses and coffee shops in New York City, however, there is the Coffee Project NY owned by Chi Sum Ngai and Kaleena Teoh, who are both Malaysian. They are vocal about spreading coffee awareness, and just opened a coffee education center in Long Island," says Tsai. "Kopitiam in Malaysian culture is a place of gathering in between meals, a place to go to with your family, or somewhere your grandpa has been going to, [and maybe his] father [before him]... so we hope to encourage this to the local community here in Manhattan and greater New York." Representing a long heritage deeply embedded in Pang's roots, the founders of Kopitiam aim to provide a hub, where people can appreciate the generations-old recipes and traditions of the Malaysian coffeehouse.

–

注意
BONMAC
MADE IN JAPAN

The Craft of Precision

WORDS
Austin Langlois

PHOTOGRAPHS
Daniela Velasco

From slow-pulled espresso in Little Italy to cheap deli coffee, from to-go cups at chain cafes on every street corner to the hidden, hipster cafes of the Lower East Side, there's a coffee for everyone in Manhattan.

If you only had one phrase to describe New Yorkers, it'd be "always in a hurry." And this is most evident in the morning coffee rush. It surprised Yuki Izumi, the coffee program designer at the *kissaten*-style cafe Hi-Collar Coffee, the first time she saw it in action in 2013.

"In the morning, people buy their coffee at the deli. Then, after adding milk and sugar, they hold the top and bottom, stretch their arm out far away from their shoes and clothes and shake with one hand."

"Amazing skill," she remarks. "The more I serve coffee to New Yorkers, I realize that many people add milk not only for the taste but also to cool down the coffee."

This caffeine-craving ingenuity coupled with perpetual impatience is what makes New York's coffee scene one of a kind.

But in a city of fast walkers and equally fast talkers, there's still space for a slower slice of life.

As latte art champion Hiroshi Sawada, founder of Sawada Coffee, located in the lobby of Au Cheval in TriBeCa, observes, "people in New York City are busy on weekdays and tend to like quick, espresso-based drinks rather than pour-over coffees that take some time to make."

From his experience, he sees more people opting for pour-over coffee while relaxing at cafes on the weekend. And to serve this growing crowd, an increasing number of Japanese-style coffee shops are staking their claim in Manhattan's coffee scene. The newest to Manhattan will be %Arabica, a coffee chain that announced in May 2020 plans for its first U.S. cafe.

TATENOKAWA
楯野川
男山
商標
新潟清酒
商標
麒麟山
不老長生千年壽

It might be surprising to learn that many hallmarks of the third wave coffee movement and the craft coffee industry—like the Hario V60, the siphon, the Kalita Wave, matcha tea, gooseneck kettles, and single-origin beans sourcing—have their origins in Japanese culture. Even much of the modern cafe experience has roots in *kissaten* coffee culture (traditional Japanese tea/coffee shops), known for its warm hospitality and cozy charm.

But this high-quality approach to coffee is just one of many such cultural imports from Japan. New Yorkers also love their sushi. Found everywhere, from Michelin-starred restaurants to bodegas, sushi is more than a cuisine—here, it's a lifestyle. It's a date night dinner; it's a grab-and-go lunch; it's a 2-a.m. bodega craving. If you're looking for arguably the best sushi outside of Japan, it's in New York City.

"Foodies from all over the world come here," says Yuri Igata, general manager of Sushi Ginza Onodera. And as such, "the level of chef skills and availability of ingredients is very high and the guests, who typically have traveled around the world, have developed an appreciation for high-end cuisine and special techniques."

Sushi Ginza Onodera focuses on traditional Edomae methods, with fish flown in from Tokyo's Toyosu market. Its care for ingredient quality and sourcing is not unlike that which you'd find in the coffee industry. Like coffee, sushi requires great dedication to quality and a skill that's honed over time to truly perfect the end product. It seems like New Yorkers sense this, and that's why they seek out Japanese-style coffee and sushi—despite being so rushed.

Perhaps it's not the Japanese brewing methods and tools that have impacted the craft coffee scene the most. Instead, maybe it's the care in bean origin, roasting, and the customer experience that have more profoundly influenced how we experience coffee today.

When you compare Japan's largest city, Tokyo, to the largest city in the United States, they couldn't be more different. However, there's no question that the inhabitants of both of those cities seek out the finer things in life, like excellent dining, impeccable ingredients, and a freshly roasted, drip-brewed cup of coffee.

–

A Love Note To Coffee and Conviviality

WORDS
Maria Belen Iturralde

PHOTOGRAPHS
Adam Goldberg, Daniela Velasco

A multitude of cafes, drenched in sunlight and teeming with the intoxicating scent of fresh coffee, line the streets of Manhattan, tempting New Yorkers with ethereal cups of espresso, warm interiors, and—perhaps most importantly—the unspoken yet very compelling invitation to linger inside for a moment.

Words like "long black," "cheers mate," and "flat white" are casually thrown around as visitors enjoy expertly crafted cups of coffee prepared by talented baristas. These not-so-hidden gems—helmed by Australian and Kiwi expats with the laudable goal of making the daily quest for coffee not only delicious but delightful—have spearheaded the latest wave of coffee consumption in Manhattan.

In many ways, New York's coffee culture evolved from immigrants, who—in fits of homesickness and nostalgia—yearned for the tastes and habits of their homelands.

Imported coffee shops and their ilk slowly populated the streets of Manhattan. In came the Italian espresso bars, the Greek *kafeterias*, the Turkish *kahvehane*, all of which came bearing their own definition of what constitutes "the perfect cup" along with their shared traditions of communal coffee drinking. Their owners hailed from countries where cafes are more than places to buy coffee; they are essential patches of the social fabric.

The advent of the third wave of coffee brought with it yet another form of imported coffee culture, one that journeyed all the way from Down Under. These new ambassadors hail from the Antipodes—the term initially used by the British to refer to the Australia-New Zealand dyad— and they've come to the U.S. bearing the coffee culture of their homelands, complete with avocado smash, colorful *brekkie* plates, flat whites, and the promise of a daily respite from the vexatiousness of quotidian life. Representing the latest wave of coffee culture in Manhattan, their cafes are pint-sized pockets of sunshine within the city—perennially bright and buzzing with conversation. They offer great food, great coffee, great company and appeal to both the coffee erudite and the one simply seeking to have a superb cappuccino.

But they provide much more than just that. They present locals with an opportunity to engage with a unique culture.

"For as long as I can remember, growing up in New Zealand there has always been this positive coffee culture and it's completely built around friends and experiences shared while drinking a cup of coffee,"

Bluestone Lane

Two Hands

TO-GO

Left: Two Hands. Right: Bourke Street Bakery

Nicholas Curnow explains. It just so happens, he adds, that, for a lot of Antipodeans, these happy memories are invariably tied to a favorite coffee shop.

Having moved to New York, he now strives to create a space where others can have their own sunny memories. "Anyone that moves away from home searches for something that offers them a small slice of the happy memories they left behind." To that end, Curnow co-founded Little Collins with Melbournian Leon Ugnlik.

Nestled between a flower shop and a jewelry store, the cafe sits modestly on Lexington Avenue. Its name is "a tip of the hat to Melbourne culture," referring to a famous street located in the heart of the Australian city. The shop pays homage to the buoyant coffee cultures of the founders' respective countries, which center around conviviality and community.

"You step into Little Collins, there's music playing and there's a familiar face behind the bar and maybe we know your name and your drink and it's just a really pleasant experience," says Curnow, who revels in the joy of creating enjoyable moments for anyone who walks through the door.

"A lot of people get coffee as part of their routine; it's something that they do every single day. When you do something every single day and you see someone every single day, it builds a very special relationship," says Curnow.

He notes that, "Cafes play a very important part in creating a space where people can have a little bit of an escape, of normality. In New York, a lot of people's lives can be really stressful, very busy, and overwhelming, and you're just really looking forward to getting out of the streets where it's so hectic. Or maybe you're feeling really happy and you just want to be more happy—whatever it is, I think people find solace in cafes."

Little Collins, which has graced Midtown East since 2013, is but one of several Aussie and Kiwi-owned spots that have set up shop in Manhattan in the last decade. Places like Bluestone Lane, Hole in the Wall, Black Fox Coffee, Two Hands, Merriweather, and Bourke Street Bakery have become popular neighborhood fixtures, with lines trailing out their doors. They brought a cafe culture from across the globe that seemed to be at odds with the grab-and-go theme that had long characterized the city's coffee landscape. This dissonance, however, far from driving Manhattanites away, has fueled the widespread popularity of these Aussie and Kiwi-owned cafes.

New Yorkers, devotees of quality and diversity, welcomed their arrival and nurtured their growth. "It can all grow in New York because of how welcoming the city is to other cultures," explains Curnow. Manhattanites with packed schedules willfully opt to stand in line at one of these busy cafes to enjoy a leisurely cup and see some friendly faces.

The cafes themselves came to embody this, welcoming any and all. Happy Bones—the sunny, pocket-sized coffee shop now located in a repurposed alleyway in Nolita—is, for instance, constantly filled with the most wonderfully eclectic group of people, each enjoying carefully crafted cups of coffee and each other's pleasant company.

"In the Australian case, we're very accessible, very egalitarian; it's kind of the background for everyone," says Paul Allam, founder, chef, and baker at Bourke Street Bakery.

Paul and his wife Jessica Grynberg (who aptly operates under the title of "Chief Happiness Officer") run the wildly popular bakery in the Flatiron District, which focuses on quality and inclusivity. Their shop is, according to Allam, constantly filled with people from all walks of life who are united by their shared love of craft coffee and phenomenal pastries. "I think New Yorkers respect and really want quality," Allam says matter-of-factly. "The mass of humanity is here and yet you can still walk a number of blocks without getting great coffee or great food, especially in that grab-and-go kind of world."

Specialty coffee shops have been well-received, Allam says, because people have gladly embraced the culture surrounding great coffee and great food.

Before these craft coffee shops became ubiquitous in Manhattan, most New Yorkers seeking a much-needed caffeine boost were likely to be found nursing a styrofoam cup of whatever was available at the nearest street cart or chain coffee shop. Until relatively recently, it was less about preference or virtue and more about proximity and convenience.

It was paradoxical—the irony of being unable to find a quality cup of coffee in one of America's most caffeinated cities—and yet completely befitting of a population that runs on productivity and practicality.

But these new-wave coffee shops have carved a place for themselves in a city already flooded with cafes precisely because they offer more than exceptional brews. They have altered the way millions of people go about a daily ritual, not by stripping it from its sanctity but by restoring it to its purest form.

It's about coffee, yes. But it's also about the thoughtful pause and the easy-going feeling that remains long after one has left the premises, the unique exchange that occurs with another when a cup of coffee is on the table.

This is not lost on Jo Black, the sunny Melbournian behind Boundless Plains in the Financial District. "I think coffee in the U.S. is often a very transactional process," she says. "I think that people are searching for that [interaction], even if it's five minutes of every day."

On any given day, a plethora of customers step into Black's warmly lit cafe and are greeted by a group of tight-knit staff members, a menu of colorful fare, cups of single-origin coffee crafted with near-artistic precision and—more often than not—Black herself, accompanied by her children who, she says, are usually found sipping dainty babyccinos.

Boundless Plains—where one is greeted with the warmth people typically reserve for close friends or family—has become a haven for coffee lovers and pleasure seekers.

Like Black, several valiant entrepreneurs have come from Down Under to present locals with an invitation to join them in a collective celebration of life's simple pleasures and New Yorkers have accepted it with alacrity.

In the stolen moments New Yorkers might have to themselves on any given day, more than a few now choose to stop for a quality cup of coffee. It is with ritualistic devotion and utter pleasure that they offer their time to pause for a fleeting moment of unadulterated joy ushered in by the steaming hiss of an espresso machine and the friendly smile of a familiar barista.

They disappear—however briefly—into a bright and airy space that comforts and invites. There is a palpable cheerfulness in the air that echoes that of the unhurried cafes of Down Under.

"They're built upon a culture of creating an enjoyable experience in someone's daily routine," says Curnow.

It is exquisite. And we get to do it all again tomorrow.

–

Patience, Passion, Devotion

WORDS
J.R. Patterson

ILLUSTRATION
Austin Rossborough

In 1624, John Donne's "Devotions upon Emergent Occasions" caused a tectonic shift in the world's concept of isolationism. "No man is an island, entire of itself," wrote Donne, "every man is a piece of the continent, a part of the main." Seriously ill as he wrote, it's doubtful Donne knew that at the same time, the Dutch were arranging to purchase the New World island of *manahǽhtaan* from its inhabitants, the Lenape Native Americans. The Dutch purchase of the island was undoubtedly one of history's greatest bargains; an exchange of beads, knives, trinkets, and guilders for prime Atlantic real estate. Quickly, *manahǽhtaan*—first as New Amsterdam, and later as Manhattan —became the center of the world, a city built on global import and influence. It wasn't long after 1624 that the piers of Manhattan Island were piled high with sacks of green coffee imported from Europe.

"The city ran on coffee," Erin Meister writes in her book "New York City Coffee: A Caffeinated History." Lower Manhattan became the "Coffee District," and was a port of distribution for the bean to the rest of North America and abroad. Four hundred years later, it remains an axis of the industry, its cafes and baristas influencing global change in the coffee trade. As Meister writes, there's a piece of the city in "every cup of coffee and every bag of beans in the United States."

Meister's book opens with the 17th-century arrival of coffee in Manhattan, the sacks of beans already piled on the pier. But that is not the bean's true beginning. It's an understandable oversight—coffee flows through our consciousness not as an agricultural commodity, but rather as roasted beans falling into a grinder, the steam and squawk of an espresso machine, and the patterns scribbled into milk froth. A cup of coffee in Manhattan is to the Colombian mountain terraces what a loaf of bread in a Lower East Side bakery is to a Kansan wheat field. Made unrecognizable by the journey from bush to cup, the beans ground for a flat white can't communicate the labor-intensive picking involved any more than the battles farmers wage with *broca* (a beetle that bores into the coffee berry) and *roya* (leaf-rust), outbreaks of which constantly threaten production. And nothing along a Cupping Chart suggests the ongoing coffee pricing crisis brought on by oversupply and hedged futures traded in Manhattan's stock exchanges. Like *manahǽhtaan*, coffee has been colonized, and its story does not begin with the arrival of the European on the scene.

Pulled from eastern Africa and shipped around the world to be grown in the verdant mountains lining the equator, coffee has always been an unevenly distributed agricultural product. Of the top coffee-producing countries, only Brazil ranks among the top consumers, far behind the caffeine-drenched countries of the U.S.A., Canada and northern Europe. This is rare among other agricultural products like beef, corn, wheat, and rice, where production aligns with consumption. Nine of the top ten producing countries of beef and wheat eat more steak and bread than anyone else, while the citizens of the top ten rice growing countries are the top rice eaters. This is not to say that coffee farmers are not coffee drinkers (they are), but that the forces governing coffee production lie well beyond the reach of the mountain terraces.

The aforementioned coffee crisis has already caused the abandonment of coffee farms in Central America, where for the past ten years, over 60% of farms have experienced food insecurity (according to the Specialty Coffee Association of America).

"The more consumers learn and understand about farming, the more they understand the nuances and complexities of the supply chain," says Erika Vonie, a coffee consultant and 2017 NYC Coffee Master. "Being an informed consumer means they can make ethical decisions on where to spend their money." The implication is that, as coffee drinkers, we are each a customer of the 21 million families around the globe who earn their living growing coffee. And that means we're equally responsible for their viability.

Though vital, awareness itself does not alleviate the difficulty of coffee production. Vonie points to the current pricing structure, which ties market (and therefore consumer) prices to points assigned by a coffee specialist during quality appraisal. This assessment, called cupping, evaluates beans systematically on various characteristics such as flavor and aroma, and assigns a valuation on a scale that slides from 0 to 100. To qualify as a specialty coffee, a bean needs to score 80 or above. While this methodology puts pressure on farmers to create higher scoring (and therefore higher selling) coffees, Vonie says that many farmers may not have the infrastructure, labor, or capacity to do so.

The physical labor behind a cup of coffee has depreciated into a mirage of hillside figures and Juan Valdez caricatures. The gloss and glamor of roasting and barista work has become the zenith of the coffee lifecycle, greatly overshadowing its cultivation on steep mountainsides, or the time spent drying on a dusty roadside. Where does this leave the Ethiopians, Sumatrans, Colombians, Brazilians, and others who are the roots of the coffee network? Can the rural-urban divide of coffee be bridged?

At least one Manhattan enterprise thinks so. In the Flatiron District, Devocíon cafe is attempting to bridge the gap with speed and freshness. Averaging just ten to 30 days from dry milling to roasting, the coffee served by Devocíon may be the freshest coffee found anywhere outside the coffee belt.

The process is similar to the path taken by other green coffee beans, only expedited. After harvesting, the coffee cherries are dry-milled (where the parchment is removed and the bean becomes "green") in Colombia, then loaded onto a plane to be overnighted to New York, where they are roasted and served. That quickness minimizes the heat, pressure, and humidity to which the green beans are exposed, preventing the oxidation that erodes quality.

That speed has been the result of operating with a narrow but deep focus. Working exclusively within Colombia, Devocíon sources beans from some 2,000 farms throughout the country, many of them outside the country's 'coffee axis.'

"We went to the most inaccessible places," says Devocíon's Colombian-born founder Steven Sutton. "The red zones, the conflict areas." Although it means sometimes traveling five to ten hours between farms, it has a payoff. "That's where the best coffee was," says Sutton. "The original Arabicas were still there. There were bourbons, tipicas, caturras, all of them untouched."

Colombia's climate allows for year-round coffee production and a steady flow of beans, something other countries can't provide. "If you're drinking Ethiopian coffees in August or September," says Sutton, "it says a lot about how old your green coffee is." While most companies are happy to sit on their green beans for months, or even years, Sutton says the wait comes at the cost of quality. "Most green coffee is around six months old," he says. "By then, the embryo has died, oxidized. You lose a point—an 87 becomes an 86."

The loss of a point on the cupping scale may not seem like much, but to Sutton, it's a matter of pride and respect. "Why lose the points? It's a disservice to the farmer and the client." There's also quality of taste to consider. While green beans can last up to five years if kept within strict conditions of humidity, temperature, and pressure, it's unavoidable that over time, aromas and flavors in a fresh bean will be lost. "If the coffee bean is fresh before roasting," says Sutton, "the characteristics of the coffee are more powerful than if it's roasted six months after dry milling. And the longer you wait to roast, the more points you lose." Deciding to use less-fresh, stored beans like other specialty coffee roasters might alleviate the pressure of relying solely on weekly imports of straight-from-the-bush beans, but that is a compromise Sutton is unwilling to make: "You charge the customer for the coffee you buy from the farmer, not the coffee you sell at the cafe."

And Devocíon is there from the beginning, acting as its own coffee buyer and exporter, roles that put it on the front lines with the farmers. It's a relationship that requires a deft hand—coffee farmers are all too familiar with companies that wave offers of cash, but vanish when times are tough. Many of the areas with which Devocíon works were once controlled by FARC, a revolutionary guerilla movement, and the potential for violence is still there. Regardless, Sutton believes it's important that no communities get left behind in the search for business. While its beans are not stamped 'fair trade,' Devocíon upholds a standard of paying production plus a premium. It has also instituted educational and social programs for the farmers and their families, providing schools with tablets, recycling centers, and courses on quality control. "Communities make coffee. If you're not there among the community," Sutton says, "you're just a cash cow. There's no attachment. We want the young generation to stay in the local areas and become leaders."

Commitment to these remote agricultural towns trickles down into the coffee. Devocíon's speed allows for the presentation of coffee just as it would be drunk on the farm, something that honors both farmer and consumer. "You can taste the sweat of the farmer," Sutton says. "You can taste that minerality in the coffee."

Bringing consumers around to associate coffee with a farmer as much as a barista will take time. Vonie advocates for the education of consumers to help them see behind the roaster. "About 70% of all coffee comes from smallholder farmers on two hectares or less," she says. "Outside of the harvest, farmers often face food and financial insecurity. With climate change ravaging available land for growing coffee and a price crisis happening at the same time, many of the farmers who make the coffee we drink daily face an uncertain future."

Agriculture will always be steered by the will of the customer; "I am a coffee drinker" holds considerably more market capital than "I am a coffee farmer." But even markets, bent far enough, can break. Farms can be abandoned, generations separated. It has already happened. And it is happening now. The streets of Manhattan are rife with the fruits of the world's laborers. In the intervening 400 years, *manahåhtaan* has become wildly more valuable than the handful of beads and trinkets for which it was traded. So too is the coffee that now plies its streets. Paying a pittance for hard grown beans is proof that as consumers we know the price of a cup of coffee, but not the value.

Of course, coffee will continue to flow through Manhattan regardless, just as it has since the city's founding. But the gap between the city that never sleeps and the farms that provide the caffeine to fuel it will need to be bridged to ensure the continued survival of the farmers. What we need to realize, Vonie says, is that "our coffee is definitely worth $4 or $5 a cup."

Coffee is not an isolationist venture—it is a drink of the world. Donne knew that isolationism in any sense is untenable, that the earth is made lesser for any clod of dirt washed out to sea. Devocíon knows it too, and the sacks of fresh green beans slumped alongside its New York City roaster are proof of that. The dates stamped onto those bags—none older than a month—represent a commitment to providing Manhattan with the best Colombian farmers have to offer.

–

Jamie Balder, Steven Hong

Let's Get a Drink

WORDS
Brian Aubrey Smith

PHOTOGRAPHS
Jean-Laurent Gaudy

Anyone paying attention to New York's dating culture might wonder if the coffee shop date is obsolete. Check any list of "Best First Date Spots" or "Most Romantic NYC Dates," and it's likely to be bereft of coffee shop recommendations. The cozy corner booth in a neighborhood brew house has gone the way of the yellow cabs and print copies of the New York Daily News.

After all, dating in New York is a numbers game in a city of optimizers: $18 cocktails at the hottest speakeasy, a reservation for two at the best Italian hole-in-the-wall, 50 swipes right per night across three apps, and now, six feet apart at a minimum. In the era of the COVID-19 pandemic, there's less room for slow-paced, huddled conversations in high-traffic cafes.

But to ask coffee shop owners about their shops' dating culture is to realize that the coffee date isn't obsolete. Rather, it has become more bespoke.

Specific coffee shops offer a specific type of date for a specific type of customer in a specific New York neighborhood. It may be true that no one is taking the subway a half-hour across town for a 3 p.m. pour-over with their latest Hinge match. But, they are walking a few blocks to meet people where they're most comfortable, often in a familiar seat at their daily coffee shop. And that's a result of intentional choices that some shop owners are making to create warm, comfortable spaces that feel like home for all parties.

Jereme Barnas opened Little Canal on the Lower East Side with his now-wife, then-girlfriend, Gorretti Layco four years ago. The coffee shop with made-to-order food transitions to a natural wine and craft beer bar in the evening. With a background in architecture and design, Layco was responsible for designing the shop.

"What we're trying to do with the shop, because we're so familiar with the neighborhood and it feels like home, is to make a place that isn't pretentious and that wouldn't be such a scene," she said.

Little Canal

Jamie Balder, Steven Hong

Little Canal is welcoming in a reserved way that doesn't call attention to itself. There's a simple wooden bar, subway tile, leafy plants, records on the shelves, and seats along the window, all things that remind a visitor of a home kitchen or living room.

"You could just roll out in your pajamas if you needed to, grab your coffee, head back home, and feel very relaxed. As a result we've become a living room that's an extension of peoples' homes."

At Maman, with seven locations in New York, the design choices are similarly intentional. The plates are mismatched, blue-and-white China, as if they'd been pulled from kitchen cabinets. The deep wooden benches at the TriBeCa location are also not uniform.

"Our cafes do look very lived in," said Andrea DeMaio, former Maman barista and current Marketing Director. "A lot of our chairs are antique chairs and the tables are just big wooden tables. You feel like you're going to someone's home and sitting at their dining room table. It's a space where you can immediately feel comfortable when you walk in, but it's also a neutral space. It's not like you're going over to another person's home where they feel very comfortable but you don't—it's like a neutral space that brings that comfort and feeling of home to both parties."

The Hungarian Pastry Shop on Amsterdam and 111th, a few blocks south of Columbia University and almost directly across the street from St. John the Divine, is homey partially by design and partially by nature.

The cafe has been in owner Philip Binioris's family for decades. A Hungarian-Jewish couple opened the shop in 1961 before his father purchased it with two business partners in 1976. The partners parted ways and Binioris took over the Pastry Shop from his father nine years ago.

The homemade pastries and cakes are as much part of the allure as the coffee. There's no Wi-Fi, tables are jammed together, and customers turn sideways to slip past one another at the door. It's not out of place to see friends or couples huddled closely over a shared plate and books.

"Clearly you have something in common because you've both come to this place, so there's some kind of common connection, so it kind of opens the floor for a potential interaction. There's something freeing about being put in that kind of proximity to other people and having to ask them to share a table and the understanding that when it gets crowded you're going to be really close to somebody... When you go to the Pastry Shop, you're getting close to somebody because you want to be at the Pastry Shop. It's an opening, it's a little bit of an opening."

"I've been married for five years and with my wife for 10, so I haven't been dating in a while," said Binioris.

"But my memory of it is that, when you're getting started on a date with somebody, you want there to be some activity around you so you don't feel awkward. So, in a place like the Pastry Shop where it's kind of crowded and there's activity and there's energy, it kind of helps keep the conversation going or it keeps the awkward moments a little less obvious," he said.

The same could be said of a bar, of course—the cocktail of energy, activity, closeness, and anonymity is similar. Yet an interaction at a coffee shop tends to offer more comfort and ambiguity. Sometimes, that's by design, and sometimes that's a result of the way customers use their favorite shops as a space for lower stakes, more ambiguous meetings. The Hungarian Pastry Shop, for example, primarily serves Morningside Heights residents and professors and students from Columbia.

LITTLE CANAL

CAFE · COFFEE · BAR

LUNCH
SALADS
GREEN TAHINI 12
KALE CAESAR 12
VEGAN KALE CAESAR 13
BEET 13
SANDWICHES
TLT 14
TUNA 13
HUMMUS 11
SPICY MOZZARELLA 14
SATAN BANH-MI 12
GRILLED CHEESE 7
TOMATO SOUP 8
GRILLED CHZ & SOUP 13
INCLUDES SALES TAX
EXTRAS
ICED TEA 3.50
TEA 4
SODA 2.50
GINGER BEER 3
ORANGE JUICE 3 5
INCLUDES SALES TAX
BEVERAGE-AIR

 Gorretti Layco

Binioris said, "A lot of people are going on 'study dates' or they're not really sure what they're doing. So they say, 'Hey, let's meet up and study at the Pastry Shop.' Maybe it's something else, and maybe it's not. It gives it a sense of ambiguity that is a kind of a little bit of protection."

That ambiguity has always been the appeal of the coffee date—a meeting for coffee is more amorphous than sitting down for drinks at a cocktail bar. While "Do you want to go out for drinks?" often implies romantic interest, "Do you want to meet for a coffee?" doesn't necessarily so—there's always the possibility that it's an invitation for a study session or a first plan with a new friend.

Even if it's clear that the intention is more than friendly, the cultural connotation is of a shorter, more relaxed situation than dinner, where there's no way out until the check arrives and the setting is more formal.

"[Our shops] are nice for a first date in that you don't have to feel the pressure of a dinner date," said DeMaio. "That can be kind of intimidating, you feel like you have to be really put together."

Layco agreed: "I think the comfort level also helps people. You don't have to be dressed up, you can come as you are. You don't have to commit to a meal. It's short, you can escape whenever... You can still have that daytime anonymity because it's very transient in terms of how long people stay and it gets so busy."

Binioris said, "You can have a cup of coffee and a piece of cake in about 10 minutes. And if it's not working, it's like, 'Alright, see ya later.' You're not going out for an hour or two-hour dinner where you're stuck if it's clearly not the right fit."

Even for shops that are able to offer takeout, COVID-19 has disrupted all of this. The quickly rotating clientele, close-quarter seating, and welcoming atmosphere that made coffee shops ideal date spots are completely lost when a truck whizzes past an outdoor table or an iced coffee withers in the outdoor heat.

When asked if he'd noticed any daters picking up drinks from the Pastry Shop since the start of the shutdown, Binioris guessed that most of the couples he observed were already in a relationship. "I'm not sure how much of that is happening with people who are just starting to date... I can't imagine trying to meet somebody now, it must be really, really hard."

Layco said about Little Canal, "The people who've been keeping us in business during [the pandemic] have really just been the locals—people who are cooped up at home, they want their coffee fix, they want to get out of the house, but they don't want to commit to taking the subway anywhere. It's really been about people who've been in the neighborhood."

But with New Yorkers becoming more and more accustomed to outdoor dining and drinking, even with all its inconveniences, cafes are hoping to see dates return (safely, of course).

When we spoke, Layco had just reintroduced outdoor seating at Little Canal and was expecting more activity.

Maman is in the same boat. DeMaio said, "I still think coffee is one of the best options for a date. A lot of places in New York are just beginning to have outdoor seating, so many people don't feel comfortable sitting outside at a restaurant. So having that option to take something to go is really big. Even if you wanted to grab your coffee at the window and walk or go to a park, I think it's one of the more ideal options for a first date."

–

Finding the City That Was

WORDS
Laura Steiner

PHOTOGRAPHS
Jacob Santiago

It was an afternoon at the very beginning of autumn, the light was hazy orange and the air still carried remnants of a warm summer. New York was bustling, per usual. It was my first time back after leaving the prior year. Now a visitor in a city where I had lived for five years, I had no desire to do any of the tourist activities. It was mostly out of pride, but also because it seemed like an utter waste of time.

My friend suggested we take a stroll, which ended somewhere below Canal Street in a restaurant on West Broadway where the food wasn't memorable. The chairs were not comfortable but the terrace was empty and we could people-watch.

"Did you just see a ghost?" my friend asked an hour into our meal. It was a reasonable question considering I had just seen the artist I esteem the most—and the person who embodies my very idea of a New Yorker—enter the unremarkable restaurant we had chosen.

But it wasn't a ghost. It was Patti Smith, in the flesh, in an oversized black coat.

She sat at a table that was on a slightly higher level than ours, which made her presence even more grandiose than it already was and asked for a side order of spinach. She dutifully organized green leaves on top of fresh bread that she dipped in olive oil. A notebook and a pen laid by her side.

Seeing Patti Smith that day was seeing the embodiment of a city I never experienced, but the reason why I was attracted to New York in the first place: the allure of its 60s and 70s counterculture. Even now, a few years later after that encounter, I still yearn for the New York that Patti Smith represents and which she so poignantly detailed in her autobiographical book "Just Kids."

I moved to New York in 2007, four decades after Patti Smith first moved to the city. And in my quest to find some of that old rock and roll energy, I moved to an apartment in the heart of the East Village. The apartment was long but mostly thin which made it challenging to figure out how to have both a couch and a bookshelf. Its peculiar architecture also earned the apartment it's name: The Hallway.

pink olive
notebooks
candles
cards
books
art work
cook books
MORE!

COMMERCE ST

NO PARKING
22 24

46

The Hallway was on a second floor walk-up on the corner of 10th and 2nd, which means that it was loud. And because I never bothered to add blinds to my room, it was loud *and* terribly bright.

After bidding farewell to her life at the Chelsea Hotel with Robert Mapplethorpe, Patti Smith moved with Allen Lanier, her boyfriend at the time, to an apartment at 10th and 2nd where she could see St. Mark's Church from her window. By the way she describes her building in "Just Kids," I doubt we lived in the same place, but I still get giddy thinking we both shared the view of the church from our bedroom windows and were lulled to sleep by the endless noise of 2nd Ave.

When I arrived in the city, the "psychedelic" atmosphere of St. Mark's Place to which she refers was already gone. The neighborhood was overtaken by trendy coffee spots and retail shops. The psychedelia of the late 60s had been pushed elsewhere by gentrification, and the city that inspired so much of her artistic work was no longer obvious. I would spend the majority of my time trying to evoke that same spirit of New York that she writes about—the corner shop where she bought fresh mint and anchovies for breakfast every morning, the Chelsea Hotel and its array of characters, the artistic energy, and even the decay.

And in some instances, I succeeded.

Smith wrote of going for "bad coffee at the doughnut shop" in the middle of the night and sitting at the shop to work on her poetry. On one of those nights, the poet Jim Carroll trekked along and took her up to a diner on 42nd St. where Jack Kerouac would do a lot of his writing. The image of Smith and Kerouac sitting at a diner in the middle of the night with a pot of bitter coffee became my quintessential image of writers living in New York. I didn't drink coffee at the time, but I chose Veselka, a traditional Ukranian diner a block away from The Hallway, as my nightly spot. My excuse was the perogies, but really, it was invigorating to arrive at the corner of 9th St. and see it packed with comedians and writers having meetings at 3 a.m. on a Thursday night.

A few blocks south, on the west side of 2nd Ave. was Lit. The dive bar wasn't precisely Max's Kansas City, where Andy Warhol and his entourage set base in the 60s, and where Patti Smith and Mapplethorpe would eventually find their grounding too. But going to Lit felt like delving head first into a sanctuary of everything I'd ever hope New York would look and feel like. I made it a religion to go there every Tuesday night.

At Max's Kansas City, the likes of Dalí, Gerard Malanga, and Janis Joplin would gather at the illustrious round table. The Velvet Underground—which Smith deemed as the greatest band in New York City—made a home there too. Although I never saw Lou Reed ordering a beer in Lit, The Velvet Underground was always blasting from the speakers at our 2nd Ave. bar.

Patti Smith wrote that "everybody passing through [the Chelsea Hotel] is somebody, if nobody in the outside world." That's what those nights at Lit felt like too—nobody in that scene was important until 3 a.m. on Wednesday. At that hour, the whole world and everything that ever mattered lived inside those beer-stenched walls.

New York is a city so vast, so rapid, so full of art and life that it's hard to define. It's a city full of mice, of commuting, of loneliness. It's a place full of possibilities. But isn't that just what all big cities are? Being in love with New York requires, in part, believing that no other place is remotely as unique as New York. And a lot of that is being in love with a place that's constantly losing itself: to modernism, to gentrification, to 9/11, to change. It's the eternal quest for a city that so many others have spoken and written about in the past. Loving New York is living for nostalgia.

–

Late Night Kicks

WORDS
Imogen Lepere

PHOTOGRAPHS
Winnie Au

Studio 54. The Cotton Club. Dancetaria. The Tunnel. Whatever genre of music you fancy, chances are that a club dedicated to it has emerged from the beating streets of the city that never sleeps. The COVID-19 pandemic caused by the novel coronavirus SARS-CoV-2 has hit the music scene hard. At the time of writing, all the city's bars and clubs are shuttered, their lights cloaked in dust and turntables have been stilled for more than three months now. There has been no official support announced from the government, and many venues are relying on donations from regulars to help them weather the storm.

The importance of clubs to New York's creative scene can't be underestimated. The evolution of music, fashion, art, and human rights is inextricably entwined with the city's nightlife, a little like an ultra-smooth remix.

During the 70s, the civil rights and gay liberation movements were in full swing and New York's music scene thriving. Every Friday night, a diverse group—multiracial, queer and straight, well-to-do and down-at-heel—headed to music-lover David Manusco's loft in SoHo for notorious dance parties. Manusco preferred to be known as a "musical host" rather than a DJ, and always played records right through to the end without any interruption. The city's DJs flocked to his apartment after work and started to mentor the big names of the future, including Larry Levan, Frankie Knuckles, Tony Humphries, and David Morales.

Many of those names went on to inspire Belinda Becker, who made her DJ debut at Area in 1987. Pre-COVID-19, she had a residency at Skylark Lounge and regularly stopped at nearby Cafe Grumpy to get a cappuccino with oat milk on her way to a gig, highlighting the contrast between Manhattan's sleek nightlife today with the LSD-drenched debauchery of the 80s.

Cafe Grumpy

 Belinda Becker

FEE
THE SKYLARK
OPEN
A
CAFÉ GRUMPY
TRY OUR
NEW
MOBILE APP
ORDER + PICK UP
DOWNLOAD IN YOUR
APP STORE TODAY!

SHOE REP
270
KEYS M
PUSH

ALTERATIONS
MONOGRAMMING

La COLOMBE
COFFEE ROASTERS
LOMBE

"When I started DJing, everything happened below 14th Street," recalls Becker. "The big names were Nell's, Pyramid, The Loft (Manusco's parties had developed into paid-entry events that happened several times a year), Madame Rosa's, Save the Robots, The Building, and Soul Kitchen." Becker remembers the days of the early 80s fondly, when New York's music scene was a technicolor kaleidoscope, where producers wove together Frankenstein beats that drew on disco, rhythm and blues, funk, rap, new wave, and dub. Dance kids, art-punk ravers, and fledgling rappers collided in an explosion of fashion and art at addresses such as Paradise Garage, Pyramid, and the Roxy.

"Once upon a time, a DJ would play all genres of music and all kinds of people came. That was the real beauty about going out. Then hip hop arrived and with it came club segregation. Soon there were venues for specific music, so crowds became increasingly homogenous. It's pretty much the same in 2020, with a few exceptions, like Soul in The Horn. Natasha Diggs' roving weekly night has an amazing rotation of DJs who play a variety of music, with an emphasis on the horn." Of course the fate of Soul in The Horn, like so many others, remains to be seen post-COVID-19.

The 90s was a tough period for Manhattan's clubbing scene thanks to Mayor Giuliani's zero-tolerance policies. These included stricter enforcement of the Cabaret Law, which was passed during Prohibition in 1926, and made dancing in bars illegal unless the owners had a costly license. The law was only lifted in 2017.

However, the younger club goers were pushing the boundaries of gender, sexuality, and fashion in much the same way as Gen Z is now. The previous decade had been characterized by deeply conservative politics, overshadowed by the threat of nuclear war and riddled with tragedy, including the AIDS epidemic. Youngsters needed things to lighten up. Anti-establishment socialites such as Richie Rich, Jenny Dembrow, and Walt Cassidy essentially played the role of ambassadors for clubs, living together in large groups and spending all day planning futuristic outfits that wouldn't look out of place at a rave on Saturn.

As one millennium slid into the next, Manhattan's clubs were squeezed still tighter. The financial sector and dot-com companies ruled the economy with an iron fist. Paradise Garage, originally on SoHo's uninhabited King Street, was forced out after residents of a new luxury development complained about the noise. The once commercial part of TriBeCa that Area inhabited was swallowed by condominiums.

Since renowned DJ Brendan Fallis moved to New York in 2007, Manhattan's club scene has become increasingly commercial. "When I moved to NYC, Meatpacking and Chelsea were stacked with the best clubs. Pink Elephant, Tenjune, Bunker Club, Le Bain, and my all-time favorite still, The Beatrice Inn. A lot has changed since then for sure. Now it's a bit tricky to find what I would consider great nightlife in Manhattan. Perhaps that has to do with getting older. But a lot of the new clubs have moved to Brooklyn and beyond because of soaring rent prices and clashes with residents."

Fallis's career has taken a new direction as his presence has grown on social media (he now has 120k followers on Instagram) and he believes that this is crucial for success as a contemporary DJ. "I got on Instagram early and just started to post what I was passionate about. My online presence has allowed me to grow my career into the corporate DJ space, playing for brands like Karl Largerfield." He has also gone on to found his own talent management firm.

He can regularly be found sipping a double espresso at Bluestone Lane's Greenwich Village outpost, which is generally referred to as the Aussie-inspired chain's flagship store as it was the first of their sites to be built

Iced
Hot
Chai
Draft Latte
Pure Black Cold
Black & Tan
Oatmilk Draft
Oat Black & Tan

Brendan Fallis (Photo provided by Brendan Fallis)

on a larger scale and serve food. After a late night at Boom Boom Room, La Colombe, also in The Village, is another favorite thanks to its single-origin offering, including a floral, medium roast from the Congo. However, his favorite cafe in the world is %Arabica in Japan, which specializes in coffee grown on the founders' small farm in Hawaii. "Waiting for that to hit this side of the world!"

However, one aspect of Manhattan's club culture that has grown since the 80s is the presence of female DJs. "There are tons more female DJs now because technology has made it so much more accessible," says Becker, who remembers struggling to lug her turntables around on the subway. "Back when I started, I could count them on one hand: Anita Sarko, Spinderella, Mary Mac, Jazzy Joyce, and me. Now there are almost too many to count. I am Rimarkable, DJ Reborn, and DJ Sabine Blaizin are all doing real work."

One of my favorite female DJs is Sunny Cheeba, who plays a delicious blend of jazz, salsa, disco, reggae, Afro-beat, and hip hop. In her own words, "the only requirement is that it's got soul." On days off, she can generally be found hanging out at The Edge in Harlem, which she says has an inspiring atmosphere. Another favorite is Silvana, also in Harlem, which serves French press coffee from Brooklyn Roasting Company in DUMBO, alongside a menu of Middle Eastern mezze.

During the pandemic and recent protests against the racial injustices suffered by the Black community, Cheeba believes that DJs have started to rethink how they connect with people. "Music has the power to educate, uplift, transcend, and spread a message. A lot of folks have been using the online club scene to raise funds and stand in solidarity with organizations that need assistance and I believe that will continue even after nightlife opens up again."

Cheeba's own Bronx-based DJ collective Uptown Vinyl Supreme has played numerous parties online to raise awareness for causes ranging from the decolonization of Puerto Rico to recognizing the legacy of Black, trans, and queer people on America's music culture. "Looking to New York's nightlife in the future, the phrase 'party with a purpose' comes to my mind. I've always made it a point to have a message in the music I play but have been more intentional these past few months. My artistry is one of my weapons and I plan to use it."

It would seem that a pandemic, soaring property prices, and restrictive regulations haven't been able to dampen the spirit of New York's music makers. If anything, those things are making them more determined to find new spaces in which to express themselves.

–

In the Business of Coffee

INTERVIEW
Maggie Spicer

PHOTOGRAPHS
Adam Goldberg, Daniela Velasco

If you're a post-Millennial, it could feel hard to imagine a time pre-third wave coffee. In several ways, Joe Coffee paved the way for specialty coffee as we know it in New York City, introducing terms (and positions) like "barista," pouring some of the first latte art in the five boroughs, and investing in a La Marzocco espresso machine before it was an industry standard to do so. Since opening in summer of 2003, the mini empire has expanded across Manhattan, into Brooklyn, and has further growth on the horizon. For many well-known and NYC-made coffee shops, Joe has modeled a path for small, independent cafes to become multi-location businesses, without compromising quality or integrity. Places like Everyman Espresso (opened 2007) with locations in Soho, the East Village, and Park Slope; Birch (opened 2009) with 14 locations, including in the newly renovated LaGuardia Airport; Maman with seven NYC-based locations; and Two Hands have thrived while sharing turf with imported outfits like Blue Bottle, Intelligentsia, and Stumptown Coffee Roasters. We caught up with founder Jonathan Rubinstein of Joe Coffee to learn more.

Joe
Coffee
NEW YORK
ROASTERS

What led you to found Joe Coffee?
It was the summer of 2002. I was a talent agent representing actors. I left what was a cliché job—a very intense, high pressure environment with nasty people who had a superficial, shark mentality. I wanted to find the opposite of that. I sought entrepreneurial opportunities that spoke to me, a coffee shop being one of them. Specialty coffee didn't exist in New York City back then. It was all about Seattle. A scene was starting in San Francisco and Portland, and friends in Chicago were talking about Intelligentsia, where people actually cared about the culinary art of coffee. There were no froo froo drinks or muffins being served. I thought, if I do this right, maybe I can differentiate myself from the other coffee spots in [NYC], which back then were Starbucks and bodega coffee.

Ultimately, I stumbled upon [what became] our first space in Greenwich Village, on Waverly Place. It was an idealized version of what I thought a coffee bar should be: great windows, exposed brick, a little seating area in front, and it was by Washington Square Park.

What was the New York City coffee scene like in those days?
In Greenwich Village, the norm was very dark-roasted coffee served from Italian-style cafes where people would sit outside and smoke and drink poorly-extracted espresso. I thought, "Here we are in the best city in the world and there's no such thing as 'third wave coffee.'" I knew what I wanted to create but I hadn't yet tasted really great coffee. I spent the next few months learning everything I could about coffee, training baristas, and deciding if we could afford a La Marzocco, which wasn't typical then.

How did you select your first locations?
In those years you could only be in Greenwich Village or below. Or Brooklyn. It was a very slow expansion geographically for us. A lot of ours was organic. It was about pioneering neighborhoods. We wanted to be the first in a neighborhood to gain the regulars and brand loyalty before others moved in. We would move in, and then another 6-12 months later, other brands would follow.

We chose to open in places that wouldn't hurt other neighborhood coffee shops but could [also] support [a new] cafe. As we expanded, we had an unwritten rule that we wouldn't go into another coffee shop's neighborhood where we didn't have the blessing of the other players. I'd rather be able to sleep and feel good about our decisions.

How do you choose locations for your coffee shops?
We have a checklist of attributes we look for: really good frontage, a corner space, good windows. Being near a university is terrific for us but also being in a neighborhood where there is residential density that can support us when school is out of session helps. Sometimes we face sacrifices if we choose a location because the buildout is inexpensive, or rent is cheap—it usually doesn't work. I don't think there's a golden rule but I do think pioneering and making sure the right population is there is key.

How did you grow from one cafe to more than 18?
I thought: we'll do one cafe, maybe two if things go really well. When we went to Grand Central Terminal, the first reaction [from the public] was skepticism: "Why would I pay $3 for an espresso when it's $1.75 at this other place? Why would I care what it looks like?" We would say, "Try it. It's on us if you don't like it." Customers found that they couldn't go back [to our competitors].

We opened a new location every 1.5 years. We had the formula down and I had the bandwidth. Then around 2010, I became a little addicted to growth. I wanted to own [NYC] and have one in every neighborhood. We were successful because we were so different; the landscape was the opposite of what it is now. Today, I still think there's room [for us] in a lot of cities.

How do you feel about Joe Coffee being perceived as a chain operation?
I associate "chain" with "corporate" and everything being the same everywhere you go. I think that every Joe is "of the [neighborhood]" and feels aesthetically different. But the training—and hospitality experience—is the same.

To that point, how do you differentiate your brand from others?
For us it's equal parts culinary and hospitality. We work hard to be the nice guys and to make our coffee and the experience accessible. Making our customers feel like a regular is as key to us as the quality of our coffee. We love when they say, "I love your coffee but your staff is amazing."

Did you consider roasting your beans from the beginning?
It wasn't until 10 years ago that we started roasting. It was a mistake in retrospect. Roasting is a completely different skill set. The complexity of it was a little daunting—the idea of sourcing, figuring out logistics, and buying a roastery. At the time you couldn't roast coffee in Manhattan because of the zoning laws.

I actually don't think our coffee was very good for many years. We didn't know much better. We were the first to pour latte art, to talk about origin. We were the first to use the term "barista" as a real profession that was front and center. Our standards were not anywhere near what they became over the years. It wasn't until other players started coming to [NYC] or early [NYC] players like Gimme! Coffee, Ninth Street Espresso, and Cafe Grumpy that ended up being [at] the fore for many years, until we started tasting each other's coffee and discussing it. We lived in a bubble. It took many years and mistakes before it became a place of quality.

Why "Joe"?
I had five names scribbled on the back of a book called "How to Start and Operate a Coffee Bar." Some of the names were horrendous: "Barista" and "Latte Land." I sent an email out from my AOL account and 20 out of 20 were like: "Joe"!

–

Harlem's Where the Heart Is

WORDS
Imogen Lepere

PHOTOGRAPHS
Marcus Lloyd, R'el Dade

While every Manhattan neighborhood has its own personality, there's nowhere quite like Harlem. The area between 96th Street and 155th Street has played a seminal role in shaping America's cultural landscape. From the Charleston to R&B, bebop to the Lindy Hop, jazz greats Duke Ellington and Louis Armstrong to dance greats such as Florence Mills and Josephine Baker, Harlem has shaped the artistic identity of America. Giants of Black intellectual and political history including Marcus Garvey and Adam Clayton Powell (both former residents) laid the foundation of the civil rights and the current Black Lives Matter movements.

"There's a certain energy on the streets that's unique to Harlem," says Shawn Batey, creator of award-winning film "Changing Face of Harlem". "In some ways, there's a Southern hospitality in the way people greet each other. To not say hello or even nod to a stranger is considered a little cold." From mom-and-pop stalls, coin-operated laundromats, and bodegas to the spate of specialty coffee shops and roasters that have sprung up in recent years, nothing tells the story of the evolution of Harlem quite like the businesses that have defined the area over the past 100 years.

Following the abolition of slavery, many Black Americans migrated north to avoid the violence of white supremacists in the Southern states and seek out new opportunities in cities such as New York. While the laws of the north were less obstructionist toward Black American rights, prejudice was rife. Most migrants were pushed into urban slums, the largest of which was Harlem. Between 1920 and 1930, 118,792 white people left the neighborhood and 87,417 Black people arrived. Newcomers bonded over shared stories and Black American culture was reborn in a triumphant burst of art, music, and literature known as the Harlem Renaissance.

A wander through the soot-smoked streets between 1920 and the mid-thirties could see you brushing shoulders with writers Langston Hughes and Zora Neale Hurston, or catching snatches of Duke Ellington's electrifying piano music floating out of the door of the Cotton Club.

SEASON
DETAILS

328

Left: Teranga. Right: Plowshares Coffee Roasters

Or if you were really lucky, you'd slip into one of the velvet seats at the Apollo Theatre on the night the teenage Ella Fitzgerald made her performance debut.

"When it introduced Amateur Night over 86 years ago, the Apollo was one of the only non-segregated venues in New York City and ideally situated to trumpet Black voices," says Jonelle Procope, CEO of the Apollo. The theatre has always been an anchor in the Harlem community and has acted a little like a town hall in addressing the most pressing issues of the last 100 years, so being closed during the recent race protests has been particularly painful according to Jonelle. "We may have had to temporarily close during COVID-19, but the Apollo will always be the soul of African American culture and play an active role in advocating for the safety, dignity and justice for Black people worldwide."

Throughout the thirties, forties, and fifties, Harlem needed advocates such as the Apollo more than ever. The area was redlined: a racist housing policy that made it essentially impossible for landlords to get loans or locals to obtain mortgages. Many simply walked away, leaving their buildings to fall into disrepair and tenants without any legal rights. After the Great Depression, 25% of Harlemites were out of work, and employment among Black Americans continued to fall in New York as other ethnicities made inroads into those jobs—like domestic service and manual labour—that had traditionally been seen as theirs.

Extremist political groups linked to violence, such as the Black Panthers, prowled the streets. The crack epidemic hit like an 18-wheeler truck. Although they had bullet-proof glass, cab drivers chose to go the long way around rather than drive through Harlem's streets after dark.

Perhaps the business that best embodies the Wild West feel of Harlem in the eighties is Dapper Dan's Boutique. It's founder Daniel Day grew up on 129th Street and Lexington Avenue and first became interested in fashion because his parents were too poor to buy him new shoes. When he opened his tailoring atelier in 1982 he mostly specialized in fur and leather. But when a man came into the shop proudly bragging about his Louis Vuitton pouch, Day realized the power of luxury brands. Like a DJ sampling existing songs to create new sounds, he began working the logos of Gucci, Louis Vuitton, Fendi, and MCM into leather coats and suits. At the same time, the cost of cocaine plummeted and Harlem's new wave of drug lords became Dapper Dan devotees, cementing the brand's status as a local icon. When the luxury fashion houses caught wind of his success, Day's boutique was raided for trademark infringement and closed down in 1992.

A born survivor, Day went underground, selling his designs out of his car and taking private commissions from high profile names such as boxer Floyd Mayweather. However, his tale took another extraordinary turn in 2017 when Gucci introduced a look that referenced an outfit Day had designed for Olympic runner Diane Dixon in 1989. After fans pointed out the similarities, the brand acknowledged on their website that it was a 'homage to Dapper Dan'. Today, Gucci and Day collaborate together, with Day working from a new atelier on Lennox Street, a few doors down from his original shop. It would seem that the best dressed man in Harlem has never gone out of style.

In the nineties, the winds of change continued to blow through Harlem. In 1992 Bill Clinton (who would later become a Harlem resident himself) passed legislation that brought $300 million in city, state, and matching federal funds to the area. Crumbling brownstones were renovated, and many sleek new properties built. "When I started filming "Changing Face of Harlem" in 2000, there was definitely a fear of the unknown," recalls Batey. "You have to remember that Harlem was perceived as a dangerous place not worthy of investment for decades. But suddenly Disney and Old Navy arrived. Banks started to open up branches and realtors began to market the area in new ways. There are families that have lived in Harlem for generations and there was uncertainty around how the newcomers might change the feel of the neighborhood." Community-led enterprises seeking to protect the area's unique heritage sprung up, including Harlem Park to Park, which continues to represent 250+ Black-owned businesses today.

Between 2000 and 2018, the neighborhood went from 2% white to 14%, while the Black population dropped from 77% to 56 %. Newcomers included young professionals from Lower Manhattan keen to take advantage of the area's transport links and students from nearby Columbia University. Others were well-heeled Black Americans drawn to the area's heritage, including celebrity chef Marcus Samuelsson, who runs the modern soul food restaurant Red Rooster.

Perhaps the businesses that best embody the new Harlem are the spate of specialty coffee shops that have opened in recent years. They serve the area's growing community of young creatives. Lenox Coffee Roaster made its neighborhood debut in December 2010, and since then many have followed, including Shuteye, Manhattanville, and Tsion Cafe. All have been designed with a modish eye and healthy respect for sourcing.

In 2019, Plowshares Coffee opened its airy second site in the newly revamped Manhattanville Factory District in West Harlem. Comparing this new site with the original, located on Broadway between 104th & 105th streets, reveals a lot about the vibe of Harlem in 2020. On Broadway, people tend to dash in and grab a coffee to go (mellow beans from the Daterra Estate in Brazil are the bestseller), while the Harlem cafe has become a social hub. "The customer base at our Harlem location tends to be a much younger and more diverse group including locals, people who work in the neighborhood, and teachers from Columbia and City College," says founder Anthony Kurutz, who has lived in Harlem since 1999. "The site has also become popular with small groups from neighboring churches on a Sunday afternoon." Perhaps unsurprisingly, there is a fiercely loyal following for their East African offerings from Ethiopia, Kenya, Rwanda, and Burundi.

Kurutz explains how the area's unique heritage informed the new site: "All of the wood cladding is upcycled white pine salvaged from the neighboring Mink Building. We've also collaborated with our neighbors So-Harlem [a social enterprise that provides opportunities for people of color working in textiles] to create seat cushions made from recycled jute coffee bags." Plowshares also works with another newcomer, West African restaurant Teranga, which opened in The Africa Center in 2019. "We've designed an African coffee program for them, and in return, their chef Pierre Thiam is providing us with Senegalese inspired cafe bites."

Grounded in the community, referencing African and Black American culture and increasingly aimed at a cross section of society that can afford to pay $3.75 for a cortado, Plowshares seems to represent where Harlem is heading in 2020. Noah Levine, co-founder of Teranga, confirmed that Harlem's history was part of the appeal of opening in the area. "At Teranga, our coffee and food is about telling the story of Africa's impact on culinary traditions around the world and that story has deep roots in Harlem. We have a diverse clientele, who range from curious eaters trying West African food and coffee for the first time to those who have grown up with our cuisine. But we pride ourselves on being a genuinely welcoming community hub."

It's this unwavering sense of community, from the cultural outpouring of the 1920s to today's socially conscious craft cafes, that makes Harlem so special. The area's taste for coffee may now compete with its taste for cocktails, the skyline may be pierced by new buildings, and the faces on the street may be changing, but Harlem hasn't lost any of its heart.

–

Monday
Thursday
9am - 10:30am

Wild Promise

WORDS
Thomas Wensma

PHOTOGRAPHS
Nina Gorbenko

I had always felt a gravitational pull towards Manhattan. Being an '80s kid, New York—the city of wild promise—was to me the place of never ending excitement. Through the movies and television shows of that time, I felt the lure of its cultural mosaic and grimy but colorful cityscape. Neon signs—glowing in vibrant pink, red, and blue—seemed like luminous guides in a city filled with glamour and thrill. Manhattan, where the lights are always on, nights evoke zesty adventure, the days stimuli for the senses.

Upon arrival in Midtown, I immediately felt myself sucked in. It had been as if the surrounding skyscrapers had tightly embraced me and opened up all my senses. Manhattan is noisy. It's really noisy. A never-ending mix of police sirens, car horns, and jackhammers. Manhattan is not just loud, but also extremely busy. Hoards of people making their way through the maze of streets and avenues—rushed, ambitious, and with a level of urgency one can only find in a place like this.

The next morning I woke up early—eager to explore the city. Leaving the dullness of my hotel, I stepped outside and felt the early morning freshness on my face. Looking up at the sky, the sun was already piercing through the highrises and I knew it was going to be another hot day.

In need of a caffeine kick, I walked into a diner not far from the corner of 40th and Lexington. Within minutes, I found myself in a booth by the window, sipping a hot cup of black coffee. Sitting there, looking out on the sidewalk and watching the city wake-up, it was then that I realized the city had taken hold of me.

That afternoon the sky was empty and bright, and the city was perfect for a stroll. It wasn't long before I found my way onto Park Avenue and began to walk downtown in search for more evocative sights. I passed Union Square Park, where I took a little break on the grass, before turning west, and crossing 14th Street. The tree-lined streets in the

CITY
MUSIC
LANE 3
LANE 2

Cafe Integral

Faith Xue, Xavier Crowe

café
integra
NICARAGUAN COFF

West Village were a vibrant green and there was the intimacy of the elegant brownstones. I walked in the shadows which gave some relief from the burning sun. It wasn't summer yet, but there was a dry and heavy heat. I started zigzagging through SoHo and TriBeCa, gazing up at the brick and cast-iron facades around me, glowing in the sun, the large windows reflecting the fire escapes in front. They produced a pleasing visual rhythm that eased my mind, evoking memories I had from television shows I saw as a kid in the '80s, and early '90s.

How strange it is to see these streetscapes and find it familiar, not in reality, but in the memory fabricated from the movies and television shows of my youth. In truth, the city that I saw was less edgy and less gritty, side-streets not as shabby and the fashion not as chic, but everything with a strong personality, quintessentially New York.

A few days later—it was late afternoon—I was walking on 34th Street after a largely uneventful day. I had come to experience a different side of the city, one that is gray, indifferent, messy, and superficial. I found the city hectic and dirty. People walking around in their own thought bubbles. The typical characteristics of New York that make you feel restless. Needing a break, I had decided on a vertical move to escape the crowded, noisy streets. I made my way up the 86 floors to the platform atop the Empire State Building. With few people around, the pastel sky slowly transitioned into the warm colors of evening glow and finally the deep blue of night. Standing as close to the edge as possible, from high up, I was looking down onto the city grid below. The illuminated building blocks, interrupted by streets and avenues, looked peaceful. Everything and everyone seemed to move slowly and calmly, as if they were completely in sync with each other.

...

Drifting through the city, New York's cultural diversity was as apparent in reality as it had been on my lightly curved television screen of the olden days. New York City is where many nationalities, ethnicities, and a broad diversity of people form a unique union. Something that is reflected in New York's lively coffee scene, where cafes and roasters are bringing their own unique slice of culture to Manhattan.

Café Integral, in Lower Manhattan's Nolita neighborhood, is a small and unassuming looking place from the exterior. There is a faded-black fire-escape hanging above the black and white facade. Once you step inside, you are greeted with a natural light filled space, plants, and friendly staff. They form a composition that feels apt with the Nicaraguan hospitality at Café Integral, which owner César Vega describes as "a warm welcome, and great service that feels familiar and casual, but at the same time precise and focused." It is that hospitality, together with the emphasis on serving Nicaraguan coffee that is sourced and roasted in New York City, which Vega wants to bring to the forefront.

At O Cafe in Greenwich Village, the colorful green and yellow exterior is the first thing that showcases the shop's Brazilian influences. Inside, an assortment of leafy green plants, and plentiful use of raw wood give the space an easy going vibe, reflecting Brazilian coffee culture—which for the most part takes place at home rather than at a cafe. Besides Brazilian coffee, Fernando Aciar—having lived in Brazil for 10 years between São Paulo and Río de Janeiro—also brought the classic items açaí and *pão de queijo* to the menu. He says the taste of the latter is the perfect companion for a cup of coffee; "I always have my *pão de queijo* with espresso."

Another example is Kaffe 1668. Owned by Swedish-born Tomas Tjarnberg, with three locations—one in Midtown, and two downtown in TriBeCa—all have a clean, simple, natural feel to them. Inside their locations you can find a lot of rustic wood, shelves of miniature wooden sheep, and dimmed lighting. The tall-ceilinged North Greenwich Street location is lined with long, candle-lit wooden communal tables bringing the Scandinavian feeling of *hygge* to the cobblestone streets of TriBeCa, as well as *chokladbollar* (Swedish chocolate balls).

...

I thought I knew much about life in this city from the moving images on my television screen. In the never-ending push-pull of bold expression and hazy gray loneliness, New York showed me glimpses of glitz and glamour, but never fully revealed itself. When the light is right, the city is as cinematic as it has always been. Broadway remains as bright as ever, alive and unreal, crowds roaming the streets through the glimmering lights. A city of never-ending excitement and pleasure—always within sight but rarely within reach. No other place is so blatant in both its lively beauty and its lonely emptiness.

–

Manhattan:

Bar Pisellino
52 Grove St, New York, NY 10014

Black Fox Coffee
70 Pine St, New York, NY 10005

Birch Coffee
8 Spruce Street, New York, NY 10038

Blue Bottle Coffee
150 Greenwich St, New York, NY 10007

Bluestone Lane
1085 5th Ave, New York, NY 10128

Boundless Plains Espresso
19 Rector St, New York, NY 10006

Bourke Street Bakery
15 E 28th St, New York, NY 10016

Café Grumpy
200 W 39th St, New York, NY 10018

Caffe Reggio
119 MacDougal St, New York, NY 10012

City of Saints Roasting Company
79 E 10th St, New York, NY 10003

Coffee Project NY
239 E 5th St, New York, NY 10003

Daily Provisions
103 E 19th St, New York, NY 10003

Dante
79-81 MacDougal St, New York, NY 10012

Dead Rabbit
30 Water St, New York, NY 10004

Dear Mama Coffee
308 E 109th St, New York, NY 10029

Devoción
25 E 20th St, New York, NY 10003

Eisenberg's Sandwich Shop
174 5th Ave, New York, NY 10010

Eleven Madison Park
11 Madison Ave, New York, NY 10010

Everyman Espresso
301 W Broadway, New York, NY 10013

Felix Roasting Co.
450 Park Ave South, New York, NY 10016

Glaser's Bake Shop
1670 1st Ave, New York, NY 10128

Golden Diner
123 Madison St, New York, NY 10002

Gotham Coffee Roasters
23 W 19th St, New York, NY 10011

Ground Support Cafe
399 W Broadway, New York, NY 10012

Happy Bones
394 Broome St, New York, NY 10013

Hi-Collar
231 E 9th St, New York, NY 10003

Hole in the Wall
15 Cliff St, New York, NY 10038

Intelligentsia Coffee
180 10th Ave, New York, NY 10011

Irving Farm New York
71 Irving Pl, New York, NY 10003

Joe Coffee
141 Waverly Pl, New York, NY 10014

Kobrick Coffee Co.
22 9th Ave, New York, NY 10014

Kopitiam
151 E Broadway, New York, NY 10002

Kuro Kirin Espresso & Coffee
4795 Broadway, New York, NY 10034

Kuro Kuma
121 La Salle St, New York, NY 10027

La Colombe
319 Church St, New York, NY 10013

Lenox Coffee Roaster
60 W 129th St, New York, NY 10027

Little Bean
111 Central Park N, New York, NY 10026

Little Canal
26 Canal St, New York, NY 10002

Little Collins
667 Lexington Ave, New York, NY 10022

Magnolia Bakery
401 Bleecker St, New York, NY 10014

Manhattanville Coffee
142 Edgecombe Ave, New York, NY 10030

Maman
239 Centre St, New York, NY 10013

Merriweather
428 Hudson St, New York, NY 10014

Metrograph Commissary
7 Ludlow St, New York, NY 10002

Ninth Street Espresso
75 9th Ave, New York, NY 10011

Pearl Diner
212 Pearl St, New York, NY 10038

Peddler
300 Lafayette St, New York, NY 10012

Plowshares Coffee
1351 Amsterdam Ave, New York, NY 10027

Porto Rico Importing Co.
201 Bleecker St, New York, NY 10012

Rao's
455 E 114th St, New York, NY 10029

Red Rooster
310 Malcolm X Blvd, New York, NY 10027

Remi Flower and Coffee
906 2nd Ave, New York, NY 10017

Roasting Plant
81 Orchard St, New York, NY 10002

Russ & Daughters
179 E Houston St, New York, NY 10002

Sawada Coffee
33 Cortlandt Alley, New York, NY 10013

Shuteye Coffee
137 W 116th St, New York, NY 10026

Silvana
300 W 116th St, New York, NY 10026

Square Diner
33 Leonard St, New York, NY 10013

Starbucks Reserve Roastery New York
61 9th Ave, New York, NY 10011

Stumptown Coffee Roasters
18 W 29th St, New York, NY 10001

Sushi Ginza Onodera
461 5th Ave, New York, NY 10017

Teranga
1280 5th Ave, New York, NY 10029

The Elk
128 Charles St, New York, NY 10014

The Bean
771 Broadway, New York, NY 10003

The Edge Harlem
101 Edgecombe Ave, New York, NY 10030

The Hungarian Pastry Shop
1030 Amsterdam Ave, New York, NY 10025

The Perch
52 Mercer St, New York, NY 10013

The PlantShed
1 Prince St, New York, NY 10012

Tom's Restaurant
2880 Broadway, New York, NY 10025

Tsion Cafe
763 St Nicholas Ave, New York, NY 10031

Two Hands
251 Church St, New York, NY 10013

Variety Coffee Roasters
261 7th Ave, New York, NY 10001

Veselka
144 2nd Ave, New York, NY 10003

Voyager Espresso
110 William St, New York, NY 10038

William Greenberg's
1100 Madison Ave, New York, NY 10028

Zabar's
2245 Broadway, New York, NY 10024

Outside Manhattan:

%Arabica Kyoto
87-5 Hoshinocho, Higashiyama Ward,
Kyoto, 605-0853, Japan

Chock Full O'Nuts
1701 Avenue M, Brooklyn, NY 11230

Gillies Coffee Company
150 19th St, Brooklyn, NY 11232

Gimme Coffee
506 W Martin Luther King Jr. St
Ithaca, NY 14850

Hemstrought's Bakeries
900 Oswego St, Utica, NY 13502

**

This list represents coffee shops visited, referenced, or interviewed on background for the making of Drift, Volume 10: Manhattan.

M A N H A T T A N

INSTAGRAM
@driftmag

TWITTER
@driftny

FACEBOOK
/driftny

WEBSITE
www.driftmag.com